15.

JACQUES LIPCHITZ

His Sculpture

JACQUES

Text by A. M. Hammacher Director
Kröller-Müller Museum
Otterlo, Holland

With an Introductory Statement by Jacques Lipchitz

LIPCHITZ

His Sculpture

Harry N. Abrams, Inc., Publishers, New York

Library of Congress Catalog Card Number: 60-10889
All rights reserved. No part of the contents of
this book may be reproduced without the written permission
of Harry N. Abrams, Inc., New York
This book is published in association with
Contact, Amsterdam, Holland
Printed and bound in Holland
Otto Treumann, Book Designer

to my wife, Renilde

Table of Contents

Text

Plates

Statement by Jacques Lipchitz

I have been asked to write a few words of introduction to help guide readers through this book. This is a difficult task for me; but to tell you the truth, I am the first one to be astonished to see what comes from my hands. Such a situation commands a special attitude toward myself. Knowing all my weaknesses I have to take many precautions, spiritual and material, before I start a sculpture, in order not to be lost during my perilous voyage. But despite all my precautions, my ship is sometimes lost in the space of my imagination. That's why you will find in my work two clearly defined ways – one built on a solid foundation, the other a kind of lyrical expansion; the one nourishing the other in a continuous flow of mutual support. Always mutual support, always, I would say, encounters. And working in such a manner teaches me also a way of life. All my human potentialities are engaged in this struggle for complete harmony.

So with me it is a matter of encounters. I have always been fascinated by encounters: the encounters of materials, the encounters of ideas, the encounters between myself and things not-myself, and the encounters of various sides of myself. Sometimes these encounters are between similarities and likes; sometimes between opposites or wildly different things. But encounters are unpredictable, and through them the fabulous may take shape. From the encounter in the mind comes something entirely different from any of the ingredients, and something that is unpredictable until then.

So I welcome the encounters wherever I go or whatever I do. I know it is easier and more "sensible" to put things in their places and to try to eliminate the element of surprise from daily life – and from art, too, for that matter. But my inclination is otherwise, and therefore it does not astonish me that during my walks in the city or in the country or when I go to museums, or when I witness events in my personal life, things which strike my eyes are entering into metaphorical relations with each other. I have acquired a complete confidence in my eyes, because again and again I have been struck with the way my eyes perceive first and more truly than all my other senses together.

I remember, not so long ago, that an unfriendly critic had said that Lipchitz would even throw clay onto the floor and call it sculpture. When I heard about it, I recognized at once that there were new encounters for me. What would happen when I threw clay down? We know that Leonardo suggested that painters study the cracks and marks on walls. What would I find? The clay cracked open in endless ways, and took shapes and contours that were never the same. And when I lost myself in the encounter with the inert chunk, sometimes I came to realize that it was indeed hopeless; but at other times the piece found a response, and a new work took shape under my hands as a result of the encounter. In the same way, I may plunge a hot waxy substance – as hot as I can handle it – into cold water, where my hands feverishly model the material be-

fore it entirely hardens, while I keep my eyes averted. My hands have encountered the material; what will my eyes encounter? What will my fund of knowledge of sculptor's materials, acquired over the years – what will it encounter?

In my most recent work I have been using ready-made objects. Sculptors of all times have used such objects – Egyptian, Chinese, Renaissance, and in our days, Rodin, Picasso, myself, with my Variations on the Chisel. Most of the time, such objects are incorporated for realistic purposes, cast in plaster or in wax, to form part of the sculpture to come, yet retaining their identities. But I have for a long time been wanting to use the objects themselves as heteroclites – that is, as something that is what it is but at the same time something which is free to deviate from what it is. Wood, strings, bones, flowers, fabrics – whatever you can think of – but translating them directly into metal for poetic expression. The objects are shapes and directions and surfaces, but now they are made to speak to us as sculpture, as pure poetry, and their original identity becomes vestigial, if at all consciously present. And I have been bringing about the encounter of several such heteroclites in my recent works.

I now see better than ever that in my whole career I have been trying to get more and more freedom in my art. I have always invited the encounter – except for a brief few years when I limited the field of my adventuring because I sought what I thought I should, rather than responding freely, with my whole being, to the world around me. I feel myself the instrument of vital forces which are everywhere and work through me, to add to the common human richness whatever I am able to contribute.

I. From Vilna to Paris (1909)

As a youth in Russia at the turn of the century Chaim Jacob Lipchitz must have witnessed events that, while outwardly of little significance, were to have a long and profound influence upon him and to some extent were to determine the main motifs of all his later creative work as a sculptor.

It is possible, indeed necessary, to describe his sculpture in terms of the formal changes apparent in it, since these formal changes are connected with the development of sculpture in Paris from 1900 onward among both the French artists and the young foreigners who had settled there. An extremely concentrated process was taking place in sculpture while the painters who had called Cubism into being posed problems of form and space that involved sculpture in a three-dimensional way.

Lipchitz' relation to the most important artists of the Cubist period thus plays an important part in Cubist development, although his own original searching, which can be described in the same plan of formal changes, is more important for the development of his personal style. However, form is only half the problem, and the unity of Lipchitz' work remains unaccountable if its explanation is sought only in the history of formal changes. It is better explained, if not wholly, when we try to understand his work as a whole. It was the totality of his human and artistic experience that formed the basis of his *œuvre*: nothing in his *œuvre* stands alone. Without ever being repetitive, each work is linked by its appearance to the preceding work and even to much earlier works. One continuous current, one invisible power supports, links, and propels the whole. Lipchitz makes neither a series of images nor a group of images. He creates an *œuvre* in the old, profound sense; he creates a world within a world.

Already in his pre-Cubist period we can discern the seed of his later style. This style, repressed in his Cubist period, was afterward to be restored and to flourish. The gradual change of his pictorial content, the virtual disappearance of iconography during Cubism, the persistent return to asocial iconography (the playing and wandering men, the music-making sailors, the acrobats, the dancers, the harlequins, and the pierrots), the appearance of an iconography of sound (harps and other musical instruments, the *Song of the Vowels*), a mythological and biblical iconography, the motifs of eroticism (fertilization and fertility, the mutual attraction of man and woman), the mother-and-child motifs—all these are patterns deriving from one world of images. It is a latent world of images in which the whole of inward and outward experience is continually manifested by the tensions released in the creative act of making sculpture.

The fact that these groups of images have undergone fundamental changes several times in Lipchitz' life makes it all the more difficult for us to explain their unity, although it gives us a clear impression that they are deeply rooted in his subconscious.

Lipchitz' mythological and biblical themes have been accounted for on the basis of his re-actions to events following World War I —the threat to mankind represented by the Nazis, the new war, and the liberation. There is truth in these accounts but no adequate explanation. In his sculpture Lipchitz has reacted to political and social events, but Kokoschka and Picasso have done likewise. It can be established that Lipchitz' reactions have their roots in the past.

fig.III His sensitivity about his race and his creativity go back to his youth. His father, a prosperous building contractor, tried to prevent him from following his artistic impulses; and the tsarist regime, which subjected Russian Jews to petty restrictions, excluded a Jewish boy from taking art lessons at the St. Petersburg Academy, as Chagall had discovered. Traveling was like-wise dependent upon special permission. Fear, and the suppression that his innate sculptural urge encountered in the small community of the family where the father was ruler and in the larger community of the Russian Empire where the tsar was ruler, provoked his cultural imagination. Whatever latent creativity lived in him and felt itself threatened saw no future except in flight. The emotional tensions aroused in him by restrictions on his freedom in the

fig.II family and in society determined his secret journey to Paris. Only his mother, who gave him some money, and an uncle, who was able to show him how to cross the frontier without a pass or permission, knew of his plan. His mother, though she knew nothing of the plastic arts, be-lieved implicitly in his future.

fig.I He had gone to school in Bialystok and, later, in Vilna. His father had wanted him to study engineering. All the boy knew about sculpture was that it must be white. The plaster casts that he saw in school were always white, and for this reason he always colored his own attempts white. He knew nothing of what was happening in art either in Russia or in Western Europe. He left Russia at a time of life when the landscape, the city, and social life had already left their marks on him. As far as art was concerned he had been given nothing—except the atmosphere of a non-Western, still almost medieval, culture with primitive social relations, the memory

12

of a glorious countryside, and the attitudes born of a firm, patriarchal family union, none too strict in keeping to Jewish doctrine.

Lipchitz was grateful to his mother, who had had faith in him and shown him the way. The profound effects of this experience were an added source of inspiration for his later sculpture, in which the mother-and-child motif caught roots. Not only in his physical birth, August 22, 1891, but also in his birth as an artist she had been the protector and guide. The only "recommendation" his mother had required to begin his artistic education was provided by Professor Ginzburg, who came to give a lecture in Vilna and to whom Lipchitz showed some of his work. Without knowing anything more about him, the man gave him an unconditional recommendation. Lipchitz always remained amazed at the ease with which such a great responsibility was borne.

His fate was thus determined. Why did he choose Paris? Merely from a vague feeling that there he would find the freedom and the atmosphere in which he could become a sculptor.

Completely without grounding in the history of art, he arrived in Paris in his eighteenth year. It was a city with a different life, with different social relationships, a city that culturally and artistically was on the threshold of great changes.

A remarkable number of foreigners who proved to be greatly talented had come to Paris between 1900 and 1910. There were then whole colonies of young Russians in Zurich, Munich, and Paris, who studied there to see how West European artists did things. * Foreigners who were already in Paris at the time of Lipchitz' arrival included among others the Spaniards Picasso, Gris, and Gonzales, and the Italian Modigliani. The Rumanian Brancusi, who began his legendary trek from Bucharest and took two years over it, was already an established academic sculptor. Csaky came to Paris from Hungary in 1910. Nadelman went from Poland via Munich to Paris, arriving in 1903. Zadkine and Archipenko were there in 1909, Chagall in 1910, Pevsner in 1911. They were not all without artistic background like the young Chaim Jacob, who had to start from scratch. He was for a time a free pupil of Ingalbert at the Ecole des Beaux-Arts, where he attended Richet's anatomy classes, but he liked it better in a small atelier and at the Académie Julian under Verlet. In the evenings he attended the Académie Calarossi. At first he was much teased and exploited by the older and more ex-

* Cf. Louis Lozowick in *Menorah Journal*, January, 1929.

perienced artists, but he picked up things very quickly. His first exhibitable works date from 1911, the year in which the allowance from Russia stopped. His motifs are those of the decorative, charming taste of his new milieu. After his escape from the pressures of Russia there was no immediate reason for rebellion; he needed all his energy to learn his craft.

However, Lipchitz' early work is distinguishable from work by others using similar themes. The group that Lipchitz made of a charming woman between two gazelles is also known in a version by Paul Manship.* The elegant loveliness of the formalized curls that characterize this charming decorative group is entirely lacking in the identical subject as treated by Lipchitz. A real passion for the plastic arts is evident in the tension of Lipchitz' group but he is still unaware of the force of his own imagination.

figs. VI, VII He began exhibiting in 1911 with a group of Russian artists at the Galeries Malesherbes and in 1912 at the Salon National des Beaux-Arts and the Salon d'Automne. He made a portrait and a nude. Rodin commended his qualities, but Rodin was not yet to Lipchitz the figure he was later to become when Lipchitz was mature, richer, and had more conscious discrimination. Rodin was too domineering and in those years young sculptors wanted to be rid of his paternalism and his Impressionism. The young sculptor returned to Russia in 1912 to do his military service, which ended prematurely due to his poor health. Impressions of Russia remained vivid. His youthful memories of mountain scenery were to accompany him to the Hudson River. Now Paris gradually revealed herself to Lipchitz. The Cubism of Braque and Picasso was developing all around him but reached him only when he had already mastered his own first problems. Diego Rivera took him to Picasso in 1913. At that time Picasso already enjoyed great authority among the younger artists. They regarded him with great respect and dared say nothing critical to him.

1913 was also the year in which Lipchitz met Modigliani in the Jardin du Luxembourg. Max Jacob was also there. Modigliani recited in Italian from Dante's *Divine Comedy*. All the lyrical and musical quality of that gifted and poetic painter and sculptor was grasped by Lipchitz. Modigliani's image lives on in Lipchitz' accounts of his gentleness and tenderness. Modigliani drew and painted Lipchitz and his wife Berthe in 1916–17. Lipchitz sat at his ease for this drawing, with his hands on his thighs and his legs apart, just as he sits even today. Lipchitz was

* Reproduced p. 71 in Sheldon Cheney, *A Primer of Modern Art*, New York, 1924.

14

also attracted by Chaim Soutine. His putting Soutine in touch with Modigliani in 1915 resulted figs.xi,xii, xiii in a lifelong friendship.

Lipchitz was not yet wholly won over to the Cubism that had now reached him. Cubism was, after all, not the only source for creating a set of forms; and he was collecting art of all sorts—folk, primitive, naïve art; metal work; ship models; the art of Oceania and of Asia Minor; Greek, medieval, Renaissance, nineteenth century Romantic art; the art of Géricault and of the Neo-Impressionists. Much later (in 1945, according to Sweeney) he drew a distinction between himself as artist and himself as collector: "If the collector likes a work of art, that need not influence the workman, nor should the workman's resistance to earlier works of art interfere with the collector's interest."

With Lipchitz collecting cannot be separated from creativity, for in collecting he created for himself a private reservoir of potential influences, material that exhibited qualities and characteristics corresponding to his creative powers. His finds in the market, at little shops, and at dealers were directed by his own latent and often unconscious formal world, which he came to recognize through the articles that he found, often anonymous or belonging to other civilizations and with their own historic backgrounds and affinities. Often he could not even define his desires, and it was apparent only afterward that he had chosen intuitively whatever at the time had active value for his new artistic awareness. In the meantime his knowledge of origin and style and ability to recognize them had increased impressively. The beginnings of new stylistic development, however, were based entirely on intuition.

During the development of Cubism the same phenomenon occurred among the group that discovered African Negro art: Matisse, Picasso, Braque, Derain, Vlaminck, and Epstein. This discovery at the same time influenced their feeling for structure. Their inner development and the stresses that occurred in it had made them sensitive to certain—generally archaic— art forms. Their discoveries merely reinforced what already was within them, thus building up their potential of creative energy.

Lipchitz' native collecting impulse was further reinforced by the example of his father and grandfather. The father is, thus, with respect to his son's artistic gifts, not solely an obstructive, repressive figure. Both grandfather and father felt a strong impulse when traveling to seek out and buy unusual objects, which often they could not identify and which did not always appeal very much to Lipchitz' mother. The house was full of the most varied objects such as sculptures (including riders on prancing horses), paintings, carpets, and also fragments and scraps of things in which he saw some beauty. This impulse was continued in the sculptor, but it was guided now by his finer and stronger powers of discrimination and was unconsciously directed toward his creative desires. I know of no contemporary who has managed to make the richly varied past that he has around him so visible, so that it represents, as it were, the collective subconscious of his era. It reminds one of fifteenth and sixteenthcentury figures whose unusual creativity was often linked with a hunger to discover antiquity.

On his journey to Spain in 1914, Madrid and Majorca came as revelations to Lipchitz and broadened his emotional and artistic experience. On the whole he traveled little: he never saw Italy and he visited Holland only to see the work of Rembrandt. Spain brought a great shock. He saw the great painters, especially El Greco, Goya, Tintoretto, and Hieronymus Bosch. The sculptor saw in El Greco more than just the painter. El Greco's expressive deformations, his ecstatic imagination, and at the same time his mystic's vision that makes no distinction between earthly and divine reality made a deep impression upon Lipchitz. He awoke to greater possibilities. He saw the bold mannerism of Tintoretto and the demonism of Goya. Whoever wants to understand the later Lipchitz should not forget his Spanish impressions, his numerous visits to the Prado, and his encounters with ordinary Spanish people. Majorca brought him in closer contact with nature. With his head full of the paintings in the Prado, and confronted by the mountains and the sea, he saw his own task more clearly. With touching assistance from Spaniards, who gave him the materials, Lipchitz was able to work there in his hotel room.

What he did in 1913 and 1914 marked, in its closed form and its conciseness, the great moment in which he positively emerged as a sculptor. The transition from a hesitatingly fig.xxiv negative to a positive position was accomplished. The single figures of *Dancer* (1913), *Girl with Pigtails* (1914), and *Toreador* (1914) are powerful, positive, and completely thought out. figs.xxiii,li, More complicated are *Woman with Serpent* (1913), *Mother and Children* (1914–15), and *Acro-* pl.19,fig.xxv *bat on Horseback* (1914) which represent the most important advance on his work of 1912. The sensitive contour of the body rendered by a flowing line has been abandoned for strong articulation into parts. The transitions are sharply accented, the melodious quality of the line

16

I

Documentation

I Lipchitz as a child
II Lipchitz' mother, age 32
III Lipchitz' father

II

III

IV

V

VI

VII

VIII

IX

IV *Lipchitz, age 21*
 V *Lipchitz, age 21*
 VI Seated Nude, *1910*
 VII The Poet and Painter Cesare Sofianopulo, *1911*
VIII *Lipchitz in 1922*
 IX *Lipchitz in 1926*
       in the garden of his house built by Le Corbusier,
       Boulogne-sur-Seine
  X *Studio of the house at Boulogne-sur-Seine*

X

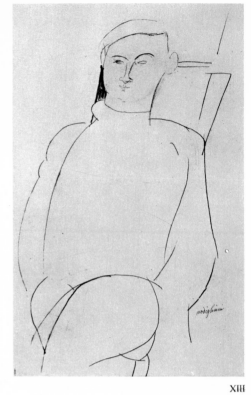

XI

XII

XIII

XIV

XV

XVI

XI Lipchitz, *(drawing by Modigliani)*, 1916
XII Lipchitz, *(drawing by Modigliani)*, 1916
XIII Lipchitz, *(drawing by Modigliani)*, 1916
XIV Front of a postcard from Lipchitz
 to Giovanni Scheiwiller, 1921
XV Back of postcard
XVI Lipchitz in Paris in 1937 with the clay model of
 his Prometheus Strangling the Vulture,
 commissioned for the Paris World's Fair
XVII Studio at 2 East 23rd Street,
 New York, 1944

XVII

XVIII

XIX

XVIII *Lipchitz at-Hastings-on Hudson working*
      on the bronze statue of Notre Dame de Liesse
 XIX *The new studio, built on a cliff above the river at*
      Hastings-on-Hudson, into which Lipchitz moved in 1953
  XX *Studio at Hastings-on-Hudson,*
      January, 1959

XX

XXI Lipchitz, January 1959
XXII The plaster model for La joie de Vivre
(1927), in the studio at Hastings-
on-Hudson

XXI
XXII

has disappeared, and a hard rhythm develops. The mass is sometimes rounded, sometimes reduced to angular surfaces.

The scheme is clearest in the *The Meeting* of 1913.* Both straight and curved lines occur. fig.XLVII The schematization leads the patterns back to a spatial unity that recalls the sketchbook pages of the thirteenth century architect Villard de Honnecourt. In Villard, also, one finds figures meeting, their legs deployed along diagonals; the triangle dominates in the articulation of the body, and rotating crosses denote movement. Villard de Honnecourt displays a dynamic geometry to which the human figure is subordinated. In an already Gothic world a Romanesque practice, philosophically based, still survived. He must have been a typical transitional figure acquainted with the Irish interlace as well as with traces of Spanish and Jewish mathematical thought in art.

Lipchitz knew the pages of Villard de Honnecourt and took great interest in this abstract foundation of appearances. One should not think of Cubism in those years as a system or a fixed discipline but, rather, as an ever-changing, even unsystematic movement into which many artists introduced individual elements, and which, moreover, was being continually pushed into further experiment. It was a new orientation of the creative spirit that looked for support or enlightenment everywhere, even in the past, to the curved line and volume of ball and cylinder at the same time as to this schematic conception of space and its dominating rectilinearity. *Woman with Serpent*, for example, is a remarkable modern reminder of the pls.10,11 Laocoön group. The so-called *serpentina* line, evident in some sculptures of Matisse—among others the *Serpentina* of 1909—is a linear conception that brings about a deformation of anatomical appearance without Matisse's changing the Impressionistic sculpture surface that had continued from Rodin, and without his breaking with his own frontal conception. Bourdelle, in 1911, created a more or less serpentine form in the female figure of *Pomona*. In El Greco, the sixteenth century had witnessed an expressive strengthening of the Mannerist serpentine style. It is not without significance that Lipchitz, who made his Spanish journey in 1914 and had been struck by sculptural elements in El Greco's painted figures, had already before then shown evidence of this from his own sensitivity. The element of Mannerism,

* De Chirico's painting *Hector and Andromache* (1917) seems related to Lipchitz *The Meeting*. In many respects De Chirico must have recalled the Lipchitz sculpture of 1913 in his own picture.

in the new art-historical sense of an all-embracing, general stylistic concept, plays an important part in the whole of the new orientation of the arts, an orientation that cannot be understood, however, apart from its simultaneous archaizing.

The diagonal of a woman's body was made by Mannerist snakelike curves into a labyrinthine whole where the enclosed forms have already verged upon becoming open forms. The development of transparency and highly stylized forms characteristic of Lipchitz' style of

pls.10,11 1926–31 is already anticipated in the arabesques of *Woman with Serpent* and the slightly later
fig.xxv *Acrobat on Horseback* (1914).

fig.19 The conclusive work of these two decisive years, 1913–14, is the triad of a mother with two children on a chair, in the manner of ancestor statuary from Oceania. The woman's torso is angular, with powerful vertical deformation. The openings between her arms, which support the child, and the outstretched arms of the child clearly have a form that corresponds to the openings in the back of the chair. The motif expresses happiness in a simple way and, as well as recalling folk art in its sentiment, reminds one of Chagall. Russian childhood memories are, presumably, continued here, and the whole work has something exultant about it. It was made in the year that he began living with Berthe Kitrosser. The curves and straight lines, the stiffening of the surfaces, the hard accents at the transitions, and the human expressiveness sum up Lipchitz' new powers.

From a tentative, even negative beginning, linked to a tradition that had become a convention, in four years he had penetrated to the sources of his own positive form world. This latent form world becomes coherent in a dynamic geometry of Spanish and Jewish origin. Villard de Honnecourt's sketchbook acted as a fulcrum and fitted in with Cubist ideas around Lipchitz. In this way Lipchitz was drawn toward an abstract conception of space. At the same time he discovered his connections with a Mannerist sixteenth century world of expression: movement, curved lines, and rounded forms appeared in his sculpture, and closed, solid forms became more open.

One speaks sometimes of "Modern Baroque" elements in the twentieth century, but it seems more exact—and Lipchitz' affinities with El Greco, Tintoretto, and the serpentine style support this view—to refer to a Mannerist tendency. This tendency was associated with notions about the mathematical basis of form.

What impression upon others was made by this twenty-four-year-old, who had already

26

expressed himself with originality and great conviction? Those who knew him well were struck by his seriousness and good character. Juan Gris, who knew him intimately, wrote to Kahnweiler in 1919 that among the younger artists Lipchitz had a great future.

Many people came together at Gris'. Gertrude Stein, Raynal, Reverdy, and the Chilean poet Huidobro, who was also a friend of Juan Larrea (later to write on the mystical and spiritual aspects of Lipchitz' work and on Picasso's *Guernica*). Lipchitz felt quite at home in this milieu; he was well versed not only in music but in literature. Of nineteenth century French literature he had read Baudelaire, Mallarmé, and Rimbaud, and he took an active interest in French culture. Raymond Radiguet and Jean Cocteau, to mention two men of letters of whom he made portrait sculptures, as well as Max Jacob, Blaise Cendrars, and Jules Romains belonged to his circle. Among the painters it was the Mexican Diego Rivera, who had introduced him to Picasso, who became a good friend, though never so intimate as Juan Gris was soon to become. Gris revered Picasso, and Alice B. Toklas notes via Gertrude Stein: "It was in these days that Juan Gris, a raw, rather effusive youth, came to Paris from Madrid and began to call Picasso 'Cher Maître,' to Picasso's great annoyance."

Lipchitz relates that, already in 1915 and 1916, Picasso was a venerated figure and that disagreement with Picasso was not well received in artistic circles even if the person who disagreed said simply and directly what he felt, as Lipchitz himself could do so well, without concealing his powers of critical discrimination. There were many discussions about basic principles; in fact a collective search went on, during and after the war, until everyone came eventually to stand on his own feet and carry on further by himself. In this period of collective search for a basic alchemistic formula for art, philosophy was examined—but no longer that of the famous Bergson, who had fascinated the previous generation of artists with his intuition but who did not appeal to the Cubists. It was more likely to be Paracelsus and St.-Martin de Lyon, an eighteenth century philosopher who propagated a set of ideas that included the unity of all religions, the value of primitive Christianity, and rejection of the central role of reason. He sought a primal knowledge and attributed great value to creative power: "All is image; we swim beneath a shade in the atmosphere of images." Such was the nature of the adjoining realms that influenced the artists who realized Cubism.

II. Encounters with Cubism

Although Cubism was primarily a movement in painting, sculpture had been drawn in from the beginning, though at first hesitantly and limited to a few examples; until, from 1911 onward, that is, at the end of the first or Analytic Cubist period, sculpture became completely subject to Cubist ideas. Art historians cite Picasso's well-known *Woman's Head*, dated 1909 by Barr and 1910 by Kahnweiler, which had a fluted angular outer edge and still respected basic anatomy; but Picasso had developed Cubist style much further in painting than in sculpture. Nadelman, the Polish sculptor, had already made geometric-form analyses of heads in his drawings of 1905. Picasso must have seen his stylized sculpture and drawings through Leo and Gertrude Stein. Archipenko also had contact with Nadelman in Paris in 1909, but one cannot yet speak of a real attack on the old three-dimensional vision. In fact sculpture was primarily dependent upon a series of archaic revivals—a series in that each artist was interested in a particular archaic style. One cannot write the history of that period while information remains unavailable about important factors in the fascination with the archaic that had grown since the beginning of the twentieth century.

Brancusi's archaic links were different from Maillol's. Bourdelle's were different from those of the sculpture painters, such as Modigliani, Matisse, Braque, and Picasso. Anything archaic or prehistoric now fascinated the painters to an extent that it was no longer a matter of individual influences but a symptom of changes in the spirit of the age. Creative men searching for fresh, new spatial conceptions rejoiced when they discovered relevant forms from the past or from non-European cultures.

Such periods of search are nearly always periods of growth, of old forms subjected to new impulses. Cubism is inconceivable without this archaizing current. For sculpture the archaizing tendency meant the approaching end of domination by superficial optical effects of light and shade—the legacy of Impressionism. The studies by Münz and Löwenfeld of sculpture made by blind people made clear the parallelism between the space conception of the blind, based on the sense of touch, and the space conception of the sighted in archaic periods. Forms developed on the basis of perception through touch began to appear in sculpture.

Only after 1910 do smooth, taut forms appear that abandoned the Impressionist tradition of a pictorially interesting surface for original forms that were more architectonic or tactile. Boccioni, the Italian Futurist, had made heads and other compositions in 1911 and 1912 that went further than Picasso's head of 1910. Boccioni also experimented with the surface, treating it more stormily, more aggressively, and with pronounced anatomical distortion. Duchamp-Villon heralded a great style in 1910 and 1911 with a torso and a head of Baudelaire, but it was 1914 before he converted the pattern, especially in the horses, into a mighty spatial rhythm of taut, elementary forms that, in its clarity and tension, signified a true transformation of space. Brancusi created his bird *Maiastra* in 1912. The endless polishing that he went in for was a refined appeal to the sense of touch; it also resulted in a maximum surface reflectivity, hence surrendering the form, as it were, to the prevailing light. In 1912 Boccioni created his marvelous metamorphosis of a bottle in space, full of a restlessness that never allowed his work to have the clarity of Duchamp-Villon. In Boccioni's work there were always nodal problems that were scarcely solved before he continued violently. But his vision had in any case surrendered the old fixed sculpture for the sake of movement in space. The pictorial contour of the closed volume has disappeared. Contour dissolves into a number of pulses of movement mounting to a peak of discharged energy.

Cubism, as realized in a number of paintings (as distinct from Cubism as critically and theoretically perceived by Denis, Apollinaire, Kahnweiler, Ozenfant, and Jeanneret), had continued cautiously to explore space in front of the picture plane. This presented the painter with many spatial problems. The Cubist theorist wanted to break with the illusionism of the nineteenth century, but in fact even pictorial Cubism could not do without the illusion of space. The fixed viewpoint was abandoned, but objects were still formed in space. This space was severely limited, but so long as depth was rendered on a painted surface Cubism continued to have an illusory spatial element. It was desired, however, to make this space measurable and tangible, not endless space or floating chiaroscuro. Thus, reliefs made of wood, paper, and other materials came into being. Picasso made one in 1912 or 1914 and so did Braque. Many of these reliefs seem to have disappeared or to have been destroyed. We continually see transitional forms arising that are neither painting nor sculpture. Archipenko used the term "sculpto-painting." Two techniques in one work of art produced hybrid forms.

In this connection one must also mention the *papiers collés* and the *collages*, which substitute for the customary colored materials such other means as sandpaper, wallpaper, sand, and wood combined with drawn lines or paint. Laurens, Gris, Picasso, and Braque made them,

30

and various Dadaists and Surrealists made *collages*. Picasso's paper or wood constructions of 1912–14 went one step further, so that relief was asserted, with even three-dimensional tendencies. The playing with space that had begun in painting with overlapping or interpenetrating surfaces was driven toward an even greater tactility, a borderline realm in which sculpture awaits, as it were, the sign to reveal itself. This propulsion toward the three-dimensional was accompanied in painting itself by a gradual contraction and purification of forms and means, a withdrawal from three-dimensional vision.

Picasso in his painting then eliminated as much as he could of the illusionary third dimension. In 1915 he produced flat works and purer geometrical forms; there is even an increase of verticalism. *The Harlequin* of 1915 has a simplicity and a lamination of surfaces that is not influenced by African sculpture, as has been claimed, but was a consequence rather of the Cubist spatial view itself, which was finally freed of illusionism.

The symbol for this period, in which the elements of painting, relief, and sculpture in the round become more clearly distinguished, is the "crystal." The rectilinear crystal that seemed to eliminate curved lines, curved surfaces, and three-dimensionality from painting did not prevent Picasso from using realistic figuration at the same time (the portrait of Vollard).

The concept of the crystal in 1915 had a definite significance for the time. For the artists it formed unconsciously a symbol of what they were looking for—symmetry, balance, and clarity. It meant the seeking of a schematic basis for appearance. Those, like the young Lipchitz, who had studied Villard de Honnecourt must at least have found man constructed according to the mystic pentagram. The geometric structure of the organic and inorganic world connected microcosm and macrocosm. Thus Cubism had some connection, however vague and intuitive, with the very old esoteric knowledge of number and relation. The crystal in 1915 had a value for the time. In Paris it was a password. But in that same year, 1915, in the middle of the war and without contact with Paris, Paul Klee wrote in his diary: "I wonder if I will become the crystalline type?" He also had a contemporary conception of the abstract: "The more horrifying the world as it is today becomes, the more abstract will art become, whereas a happy world produces nontranscendental art." This is at least placing the crystal in the world. Klee for that matter asks himself: "Can I die then, I crystal?" "I crystal"—in Paris no one would have put it quite that way. Jules Romains apparently asked Lipchitz later, not without some suspicion and reserve: "But what do you actually know about the crystal?" Romains transferred doubt to the sculptor. The crystal, which did not depend on organic growth but on molecular arrangement and which obeyed a different rhythm, was abandoned as soon as contact was resumed with living organisms and another, more dynamic rhythm sought also for another geometric principle and another balance than that of the crystal. These forces formed the basis of Lipchitz' work in the years 1915 to 1917.

Critical theorists like Apollinaire, whose main interest was painting rather than sculpture, considered sculpture to belong to the realm of architecture: "As soon as the elements that make up a piece of sculpture no longer find their justification in nature, this art becomes architecture," he said, and he repeated the remark with variations. The painters who practiced sculpture incidentally did not achieve this architectural quality in sculpture. In their reliefs, *papiers collés*, and constructions they remained pictorial. It was for the thoroughgoing sculptors to achieve it. The twenty-three-year-old Lipchitz in 1914, during and after his Spanish journey, had in a concentrated, clear, and positive way established his own archaistic, Mannerist, geometric vision of space in a number of works. The wartime atmosphere of Paris certainly affected him. One can best learn about the atmosphere in which the non-French then lived from Gertrude Stein's writings. The collective effort and interchange of ideas of French and foreign artists involved in Cubism had already suffered a severe blow in the departure for the front of the Frenchmen Léger, Duchamp-Villon, and La Fresnaye, and of foreign volunteers such as Csaky and Apollinaire. Those who did not have to do military service remained intent at work.

Gradually Lipchitz was drawn more and more into the realm of Cubism. With him there was no longer any question of a negative attitude; he knew what he wanted and his affinities were clear. For instance, for a time he had his atelier next to Brancusi's. Naturally, he knew his neighbor; but no bond, either personal or artistic, grew between them. His was a different path. Already he had realized that for him Brancusi's beginnings lay outside the examples that inspired him.

In 1915 and 1916 he produced constructions that could sometimes be dismantled and for which he used wood. They have a remarkable verticality and strictness of line; except for a few curves the lines are straight, and volume scarcely exists. He worked with surfaces or thin strips, and thus his forms, no longer enclosing volume, were like a variety of planes crossing one another in different directions. Figure representation did not disappear, but it no longer had any value except as a point of departure for clearly articulated spatial rhythm.

The year 1916 brought, on the whole, very narrow, vertical, almost Gothic figures in which the figurative point of departure lies a long way off for the viewer. In the hooded, standing, stone figure of 1916 (later cast in lead) Lipchitz seems to prove Apollinaire's thesis that fig.xxix makes architecture of sculpture that abandons nature. The surfaces, cut off by a pyramid and slanting upward in reverse perspective, define an abstract form with a cleft in which his vertical array of geometric bodies nestles almost shyly. It is an inward-turning, ascetic art that, primarily, reduces volume to a minimum and no longer tries to tie experience of space to the front or rear of a form. Space is no longer shut out but conceived in a tactile way. The image itself is the definition of the space. In *Man with a Guitar* Lipchitz even introduced a round opening that pl.22 bored through the enclosed volume of the figure. Completely illogical from the point of view of representing the body but revolutionary in form construction in that undefined space is now drawn into the definition of the sculpture, it thus demonstrates that space is not only outside but inside the sculpture.

Lipchitz still recalls the emotion that thrilled him physically through and through when he bored through the sculpture, so opening up what had been enclosed. Here was the beginning of transparent sculpture. The open aspect of sculpture, as the forms of the body describe it by their attitude to another body, by a raised arm, or by the positions of the legs, had already been given so much attention by Rodin that insight was possible, if only vaguely, into the potentialities of open form. Archipenko consciously went further than Rodin, but his work remained in essence the stylization of open forms bounded by the contours of the body. With Lipchitz something quite different was happening. The public found it strange to bore through a figure, even though Cubist. It was indeed integration of space as such in the sculpture, but it was more than simply an aesthetic and artistic experience. In this way, a cosmic symbol was being restored unconsciously: pierced stones had signified, even in prehistoric times, the divine womb. Boring through signified regeneration. Fifteen years later, in 1931, Henry Moore and Barbara Hepworth considerably extended these potentialities. Barbara Hepworth also once described the emotions that accompanied making a hole in the material. For her it was primarily the penetration of light into the darkness of the material. Lipchitz did not continue with it. Not until 1926 and then in a totally different way, did transparent forms suddenly acquire a major place in his *œuvre*, but he had laid the foundations in 1916.

This act gave signs of a concentration of all his powers, of the sculptor as much as of the thinker. Abstraction must have had great power in those years, a power also employed in seeking a philosophical explanation for one's actions. Juan Gris, who was very intelligent, became Lipchitz' great friend, and their exchange of ideas certainly exerted a mutual influence. They remained together even when they left Paris in 1918. Before anyone else had understood that the bombs that fell on Paris did not come from airplanes, Gris had already urged Lipchitz to leave because he had thought of other means of bombardment. He had a house in Beaulieu, and in 1918 Josette and Juan Gris and, later, Marie Blanchard, Metzinger, and the Lipchitz couple fled to Beaulieu from the "Big Bertha" cannon threatening Paris. In the autumn they all returned. They had gone for walks, swum, carried on discussions, and worked. Lipchitz had

pl. 4, 5 no materials there for sculpture and was obliged to make drawings and reliefs.

pls. 25, 27 Juan Gris also started to produce sculpture. Kahnweiler says that his most thoughtful sculpture
pl. 35 was produced in 1918, the year in which he saw a great deal of Lipchitz. In 1923 Gris made playful colored figurines from sheet iron. In his sculpture Gris remained typically a painter. In his metal figurines he began with a surface that he cut out and then bent. The third dimension was produced by bending but the point of departure was the flat surface.

In this atmosphere of group thinking and working Lipchitz was always a sculptor in the absolute sense. He began not with a surface but with an imagined third dimension, so that when he attempted reliefs in Beaulieu it was quite a different sort of relief from those produced by the painters.* The painters hankered after a tangible third-dimensional element that they achieved by surfaces parallel to the picture plane; the sculptors retreated from the fullness of three-dimensional imagination to a half-way stage. Thus Lipchitz' relief was always the product of a drive that had to impose three-dimensional limitations upon itself. The motifs are still lifes, as were often the painters' motifs also. Lipchitz deepened the surfaces, the objects

pl. 36 having light curves. Between the lowest and the highest there was a great amount of shadow, which continually betrayed the artist accustomed to think in three dimensions. Sometimes he

* Brion, p. 147, totally misunderstands the differences between, and the significance of, the reliefs.

34

used color. Color was experimental in the relief; Lipchitz wanted to see if color increased or decreased the spatial effect. He became attracted by color and drawing, but he did not want coloring or drawing to distract him from his sculpture.

The sculptor in him controlled the color. With Picasso it was the other way round—the painter in him restrained the sculpture. Picasso very often painted sculpture, and one can feel in his actual sculpture that its origin was in painting. The undeniably powerful plastic urge in Picasso was restrained and pervaded by a painter's urge that increased almost continuously in its potency. In 1917 there occurred a remarkable change in Lipchitz' work: strict verticalism was broken and he produced works on the theme of musicians and bathing women, who also feature in Picasso's painting. As far as content is concerned the themes of Cubism no longer have any direct literary connection—they are really pre-iconographic themes of simple, every-day objects, such as Chardin treats in his still lifes and interiors. As a group the Cubists chose the same things: tables, pipes, glasses, carafes, bottles, cups, knives, tablecloths, tobacco pouches, newspapers, musical instruments, playing cards, bread, grapes, and occasionally flowers. Among human figures they chose those on the periphery of the community—by preference acrobats, dancers, musicians, and nudes. There is no personal relation with the objects or figures. The objects are archetypes, symbols of a world that can be recognized in its simplest shapes. Although Lipchitz changed stylistically in 1917 his themes remained those taken from pl.26 the collective property of the Cubists—pierrots, musicians, and women bathing. The zigzag pl.27 rhythm and restlessness remind us of Boccioni, although the resemblance is superficial. With Boccioni every form terminates with an aggressive point and in many places the movements collide, whereas with Lipchitz every subordinate movement is completely resolved in plastic terms and kept simple. There is baroque movement only in the construction. The architectonic and static elements of 1916 are first replaced by a dynamic element and then synthesized with it in 1918, a synthesis with more volume and richer and more lively detail. The figuration becomes more concrete. Reliefs continued to play a part, for the richer and more variedly treated subdivisions in otherwise robust wholes are the fruit of his experience with reliefs. The transition from static to dynamic was distinguished by the search for a basis other than that of the crystalline world. Rhythm in space took on the structure of growth. The picture was developed out of joints that support and propel one another forward. The *Seated* pl.29

35

pl.30 *Bather No. 3* of 1917 is the best example, the *Bather* of 1923–25 the completion of the process. Between 1917 and 1925 there are clearly visible fluctuations between the attraction of symmetrical balance in an abstract world and of asymmetrical balance in an organic world.

pls.34,30 Sometimes the curve won (*Seated Man with Guitar* [1922]). In the *Bather* Lipchitz produced a shape without sharp corners, more flowing, built up from several large joints, and growing out of a vital geometric rhythm.

This variation of stress breaks with the earlier rectilinear quality. Between these two centers of tension he found room for portrait heads of members of his circle between 1920 and 1922:

pls.31,32 *Gertrude Stein* (1920), *Radiguet* (1920), author of *Le Bal du Comte d'Orgel*, who died young, his wife *Berthe* (1922), as well as of Cocteau, Gabrielle Chanel, and Jacques Le Mée.

It is well known that Lipchitz did not regard these portraits as sculpture. He did not deny

fig.VII that the heads he made between 1920 and 1922 were greatly improved over those of 1911 in liveliness, plastic structure, and finish. They represent, moreover, a conception which does not agree with that on which the heads by Despiau were based. Where Despiau, with his fine, rather loose modeling, still connects the psychological portrait with an old tradition that was revived through archaism, the portrait belonging to the period of the psychological novel, Lipchitz in his portraits is recognizably younger, freer, and more direct, and more powerful in form, belonging to another social milieu.

Lipchitz, in the fourteen years from 1911 to 1925 that he had now been at work, had laid the foundations for what was to follow. If we cannot understand his later work as having grown organically out of his previous work and as connected with it, we miss the struggle and its meaning. The connectedness of his work indicates the presence of active laws behind his creative life.

During this time he also became aware of his relation as sculptor to his material. He learned not only modeling in clay but also stonecarving, and by engrossing himself in bronzecasting he knew what was technically possible in that medium. His program of revitalizing sculpture included, among other things, carving the work himself as a protest against the tendency to let assistants model forms, a tendency that was enfeebling because sculpture no longer arose from meeting the resistance and character of wood and stone. And yet Lipchitz had the courage to stand by his own viewpoint with an outspoken preference for bronze.

36

XXIII

XXIV

XXV

XXVI

XXVII

Stylistic development

XXIII Woman with Serpent, *1913*
XXIV Dancer, *1913*
XXV Acrobat on Horseback, *1914*
XXVI Head, *1915*
XXVII Bather III, *1917*

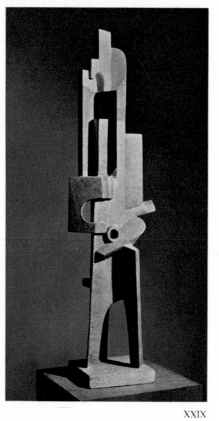

XXVIII

XXIX

XXX

XXXI

XXXII

XX

XXXIV

XXXV

XXXVI

XXXVII

XXXVIII

XXXIX

XL

XLII

XLIII

XLI

XLIV

XLV

XLVI

XLI Return of the Prodigal Son, *1931*
XLII Prometheus Strangling the Vulture, *1943–44*
XLIII Spring, *1942*
XLIV The Joy of Orpheus, *1945*
XLV Sacrifice III, *1949–1957*
XLVI Femme Fleur, *1956*

He had worked in wood and stone, but he employed assistants when Léonce Rosenberg improved his chances with a contract in 1916. After certain experiences he broke the contract four years later and bought himself free. In the meantime the dislocation of an arm caused him to limit the amount of carving he did himself. This was not the only reason, however; he was not the sort of sculptor who derives form from the stone or block of wood itself. His form assumed a shape that arose from tensions in his inner self. By preference, this self-realization he sought in the rich potentialities of bronzecasting, which he left only in part to others and which he knew so well that he conceived his work in terms of that technique. Thus the casting was not for him a translation by somebody else from hand-modeled clay, according to the practice of the nineteenth century. The clay model in his hands was directed entirely toward the consummation in metal. This was especially true after 1925, and in fact, from then on, he drafted in bronze.

III. The transparent period (1925–26) and the "Song of the Vowels" (1931)

After the scheme of organic growth began definitely in 1925 to dominate Lipchitz' work the discipline of Cubism was relaxed. A new center of tension began in the formation of his images. The positive period of thorough Cubism was followed by a negative period and the emergence of new orientation. This new orientation became negative through the relaxation of Cubist order and was made positive by Lipchitz' urge to express suppressed and dormant powers.

I have already remarked that in 1913 and 1914 the S-line, which is a Mannerist element but which in no way dominated his Mannerist work, appeared briefly but strikingly. This expression of movement was too violent not to be transitory, and in 1925 and 1926 it reappeared in a new way. In the early period, the S-line was still bound to the mass of the physical, anatomical form. In 1935 Lipchitz discovered spatial rhythm, recognizably as a result of his experiences in abstraction, to make the mass lighter and more transparant by reducing it. The geometric rhythm took on more the scheme of a labyrinth (*Acrobat on a Ball*, 1926, *Circus*, 1927) or of an arabesque. It followed a figuration, but was so free and so linear that it became a writing in space. The rhythm had become organic and full of dynamism.

In 1925 he got Le Corbusier to build an atelier and house for him in a little side street, then figs.IX,X still deserted, at Boulogne-sur-Seine, near Auteuil on the outskirts of Paris. The years of his great problems were almost past, and he now sought to liberate himself from the city and live close to the edge of nature. He chose the architect who had played a part in Cubism and who was gradually to reveal strong plastic qualities in his architecture. Although not a complete success, the atelier and house were an immense relief to Lipchitz. The glorious landscapes of his childhood in the little town of Druskieniki, with its harmonious hills; a river, the Niemen, which he knew in its entirety from swimming and rowing; lakes abounding in fish; woods of pine and fir, and oak—all this had never deserted him. He took them everywhere with him, and he wrote that it was this persistent homesickness in Paris for trees and rivers that made him decide to have a house built in Boulogne as soon as his means allowed.

The transparent sculptures of 1925–26 evolved from line and surface into space. In a certain sense they are inconceivable without the precedent of the reliefs. The lines have thickness and sometimes broaden into strips, but continue to create an impression of movement in space with a minimum of volume. At the same time, however, Lipchitz found very simple

43

figures combining the rudiments of open space with more voluminous strips: a lightly vaulted surface bounded by a sharp line, which, like a hieroglyph, writes a figure in space. They are signs that were developed from closed volumes, as we see from sketches in clay, and through practice with transparent sculpture were brought back to open forms. These forms were true aspatial arabesques expressing, with line, volume, and open space, a core of human appearance.

Between 1926 and 1930 curved forms and lines gain on straight lines. In 1922 Lipchitz fig.xxxiii undertook to make firedogs for the Louis Quinze home of Mlle. Chanel. Although with his orthodox Cubist conceptions he was unused to such contracts, it seems that the motif of a recumbent woman conceived in relief form for firedogs was a new and delightful experience for him. From that moment on, curved lines and forms began to increase in his imagination. With this there grew also an organic sculptural scheme, forcing inorganic and geometric elements aside. Until 1922 figures rose from a virtually closed, powerful base. Then, on pls.43,33 several occasions, the base opened, as in *Ploumanach* (1926), the *Seated Man* (1925), and pl.36 the standing relief *Musical Instruments* (1924). *Ploumanach* clearly derives from the relief style, the studies for the firedogs (1922), and the open figurines (1925–26).

In the summer of 1925 Lipchitz enjoyed the Breton countryside with its old prehistoric stone monuments. Filled with the sea, the beach, the women bathing, and the old stones, pl.43 he made the fine, simple image of *Ploumanach*. The female figure is contained in the hollow of the oval as in a shell. This work, together with a few others in the coming years, reminds one in a way of old Chinese bronzes from the Han dynasty. There, too, undulations grew rife, and the animal figures were full of curves and large in their formal tensions, even when the scale was small. Moreover, they had a symbolic significance for which Lipchitz was also unwittingly reaching. The symbol in the art of his time was not a collective or traditionally accepted symbol, but it belonged even less to the intellectual equipment of the individual. In the subconscious it always remains a collective property but, as such, hidden. In the artistic world collective watchwords such as "crystal" arose and became common in the Cubist period. One need only examine Gleizes or Ozenfant to be aware that for many it performed a definite function. In Lipchitz' case the symbol of the crystal is displaced by the symbols of the plant and animal world. It was as though the age-old memories of paradise had come

44

into the open. The male and female in their desire for union, the rhythm of their meeting, the opposition of contraries, and their solution in a single form composed of a duality, also changed his severely vertical art into an art of recumbent, undulating forms with rising and falling movement.

He now arrived at a period of growth and of positive sculptural symbols. We should be on our guard against the idea that pictorial content, communicable in words, could be translated into his sculptural symbolism—his work has nothing to do with verbal symbols. Sometimes the linguistic character of sculpture is employed in a literary or philosophical connection.* For lack of a better term the general content of the sculpture form is left vague or dangerously confused with ethical, mythological, or poetic meaning. Sculpture is never a translation, and one can no more conceive its origin apart from a certain medium for form than one can any other variety of expression. Sculpture depends on the senses of sight and touch, not on the instrument, language, employed by contemplative reason. Sight and touch are not descriptive but formative organs that perceive directly, as forms, what would be incommunicable as language. The symbolic aspect of these forms is not in their explicit messages but precisely in the incommunicable content that they evoke like a second world. If Lipchitz unconsciously sets about creating symbolic forms it means that these belong to two worlds. The visible and tangible world renders this other world recognizable. Those who insist on speaking of a language may do so provided they think of a prelogical language of symbolic forms that almost constitute language but are kept at the individual and sensory level and never become social and conceptual.

Lipchitz' sculptural symbols are so purely sensory, so far from intellectual concepts that even in his orthodox Cubist period he was completely pre-iconographic; and the vigor with which he freed himself from orthodoxy at the same time charged the act of summoning the creative power of the visual and tactile senses—which is the clearest proof that the senses are not merely receptive but active and formative. Abstracting all forms to sense-bound terms, he developed a different rhythm in which male and female play an important role. The symbol of fertilization and fertility arose, the rhythm of union of the two halves of life. In this period pl.47 he wanted to conquer death with life. The terror of death was not dissipated, but the urge to pl.49

*Among others, Juan Larrea in a thoroughgoing lyrical and mystical consideration of Lipchitz, *College Art Journal*, 1954, vol 13, no. 4, p. 251.

surrender himself to life gained a violent, heavy, and magic emphasis, an evocation of paradise that suggests memories of the plant and animal world. The plant and animal world absorbed the human world: the three domains came together so that the imagination of the observer formed a new pattern that came creeping out of the jungle within us, from the grottoes and vegetations of our dreams and the prehistoric landscapes submerged in our unconscious.

In 1927 his good friend Juan Gris died. Lipchitz carried the bier with Picasso, Raynal, Kahnweiler, and his son Georges.

His father died in 1928, his mother in 1934. Between these two years a dear sister, Genia, much loved by her brothers, also passed away, one of six children of a family that always had been closely attached and of whom Jacob Chaim was the eldest.

pls.49,48,47 The first studies for *The Couple* date from 1928, preceded by the *La Joie de Vivre* in 1927. After 1921, and in an increasing degree from 1926 onward, he was busy with a garden statue, which was finally completed in 1930. These three important works depend on the opposition pl.45,46 and union of two patterns in a single interwoven form. The *Figure* was at first single up to 1926 and then constructed twofold from two interpenetrating joints placed at right angles pl.43 to each other, combining in a fourth and uppermost hollowed oval form, as in *Ploumanach*. The advancing and then retreating movement of the S-form is more apparent in the sketches than in the final form. At the base lies an imaginative form belonging to a wordless train of thought, one of those remarkable patterns that are continually constructed out of two elements. Without its being necessary for a moment to assume that the artist was consciously aware of them, one knows that history has witnessed similar art forms in the past. The artist's spiritual make-up must have been related to those non-Renaissance cultures. Representation of the opposed movements of animals and men who lose themselves in their antagonists and form a junction or nodal point in one intertwining vision was already known in Mesopotamia but came to Western Europe primarily from Irish miniatures and Roman sculpture. A *Trinity* by Joachim de Flores (reproduced by Jung in *Aion*) has joints, junctions, and terminations of the up-and-down movement like those of Lipchitz' garden figure. Lipchitz, however, fits two such movements into each other, and his approach is not illustrative but structural. That rhythm is anchored in him; it is already latent in the cleft of the standing figures where we can see a rhythm of divided forms. Originally the garden figure of 1921 was conceived with the *Ploumanach* motif of a

46

recumbent woman, which then wholly disappeared, to be replaced by a mask with African, pls.45,46
magic, threatening eyes. The work became a shape on the edge of humanity, like an ancestor
statue or a spirit, an exorcising spirit who wants to preserve life and avert death. No wonder
the lady who commissioned it could not bear the sight of it in her garden. During the years
in which he was working on it the sculptor had, on his own account, paid no attention to what
other people discovered in the shape: he was primarily concerned with the construction.
There is unquestionably a tangibly different aura from the form than in the period of Cubist
constructions. The shape is clearly almost a man or more than a man in a simple structure that,
with its dual elements, inhabits an in-between world and is thus a symbol. The split world has
banished the earlier single world. The themes are fixed on the age-old motifs of the mother and
child, the return of the prodigal son, grouped around the central motif of *The Couple*, called pl.49
Composition in 1929.*

Elie Faure wrote that at first sight he saw it as a tortoise, a harmonic monster from a vanished
past that rose from Lipchitz' subterranean reality with a new logic of its own.

This clear dualism, which is mastered in the formal conception but not abandoned, must also
be connected to the Jewish conception of the duality of light and darkness, of good and evil,
of harmonized but uncanceled opposing forces. It is typical that the component parts of the
principal form—an eye, an ear, an arm, a knee—indeed flow out of it but form no subtle,
smooth transitions. Each part has its own form life. The interior space thus gains also a new
closure, as in a room that is lived in.

Lipchitz now created Romanesque curves in the inmost part of *The Couple, Mother and Child*, pls.49,51
Return of the Prodigal Son, and *Jacob Wrestling with the Angel*. Transparent sculpture still contin- pl.50
ued almost playfully in the labyrinthine figures that are indisputably connected with Mannerist
stylistic phenomena *(Melancholy*, 1930, the graceful *Chimène* of the same year, and *The Harpists)* pls.42,53
and disappeared in the larger sculptures but changed through the greater fullness of the volume.
That greater fullness caused a greater tension with respect to the openness now fused into the
volumes that give space a core. Space no longer goes freely through this openness but comes
organically to live within it.

Lipchitz has often spoken of the architectonic element in his work. That, too, was innate in a

* See illustration in *La Renaissance*, June, 1930.

period that, after a disintegration of sculpture and architecture, had to reach out to new orientations. One does not mean by this that old dictatorship of architecture over plastic form but a monumentality that can, physically and metaphorically, accommodate sense and sight when detached from a piece of architecture. Kurt Schwitters, the Dadaist, essayed remarkable sculptures in which one could literally live as in a piece of architecture. Picasso dreamed in 1929 of never-realized house-high sculpture on the Mediterranean that could be related to architecture.

Lipchitz did neither the one thing nor the other. As we follow him in his evolution we experience the birth of a human shape in the space for that shape, a space that becomes different as soon as the man appears in it. His shape appears out of a prehuman space. Lipchitz' work of 1929 and later could never have become a new organic form if he had not understood the genesis of the human shape. His spatial imagination has the power to remind of a prehistoric space, an original darkness in which touch was the only chance of knowing form before form in the light impinged upon all the senses. It is the recollection of this forgotten original darkness that gradually comes to consciousness in his work. He becomes aware of his own darkness and hence of the darkness of the world.

A child as heavy as that Child whom Saint Christopher carried over the water pounces on the pregnant mother; the prodigal son pounces on the mother; Jacob wrestles with the angel; and in essence the scheme remains the same. In every case there is a return to an original source. A distant memory of an older land, of the mother's womb, of a dream, has become active, and in the reunion of the two shapes unity is temporarily restored in a symbol. The total form stands in a mighty light but the two halves enclose an equally mighty and beautiful darkness. Its difference from nineteenth century sculptural darkness is that this was forced away and shut up as an unknowable and unattainable factor in a closed volume. The second dark element, in the later sculpture of Lipchitz as well as in others, is an open, accessible, and tactile darkness in which the sense of touch can regain its ancient reality. What Lipchitz made between 1926 and 1931 brought with it all the shuddering of a creature that feels in the light the approaching flood of an age-old darkness.

48

The "Song of the Vowels"

The peak of the change in his work, under the stress of the slow birth of the humanlike shape, is the *Song of the Vowels*. In 1928 he produced this tumultuous labyrinth of curving lines on pl.54 the theme of the harpist. With the increasing fullness of the volume the harp gained the strength of wings and the harpist became deformed with it into a birdlike creature (1930). pl.53 The mother in the *Mother and Child* changed into a figure that was almost a bird. Lipchitz pl.51 possessed great powers of metamorphosis.

In *Mother and Child* the mother has no hands but she does have feet. The raised face has no mouth, as in some Negro masks, whereas the eyes and nose are powerful to the point of violence. The child has huge heavy arms. As in *The Couple*, the back is muscular and stretched pl.49 tight like an animal's. The whole has the threatening aspect of a monster and the despairing quality of an animal. Lipchitz actually created a fabulous being in which the demonic elements of vital human impulses restore their connection with the animal kingdom. Too mighty in its form and too forceful in its expression to be a game, this conception is distinguished from the gargoyles of Gothic art or Mannerist grotesques. In the earliest civilizations religious feeling needed the worship of animals rather than of human shapes, and men feared what was greater or stronger than themselves. Assyria created mixed beings. In the twentieth century it is not the community but the talented individual that must dredge the layers of the subconscious to revive the symbolic pattern.

The *Song of the Vowels*, which had its origin in the impressions that the harps in the Salle pl.54 Pleyel in Paris had made on him, belongs to the same family. Now the sculptor is profoundly aware of the primal symbolic significance of the harp; he thought of an old Egyptian prayer that was so entitled. The symbolism of the harp goes even further. African Negroes regarded the harp as related to the loom. They called on its weaving of sounds for aid against the chaotic terrors of the world. The word that the harpist used before he began his playing was evocative. Gregorian music in the fourth century knew the melodic ornamentation of a final syllable. The singer who wished to express his jubilation started to sing the Alleluia without words. In Romanesque churches the Alleluia of the gradual was followed by a long vocalization of the vowel "a." It can hardly be a coincidence that the sculptor chose as motif just such an untranslatable sound of jubilation. Here, too, in the face of the terrors of life and the world, an opposing power was sought unconsciously.

49

IV. The metamorphosis and mythological realism

Lipchitz' ability to metamorphose forms continued to reveal itself around the conscious motifs. The transparent sculptures were already a sign that his relinquishing of Cubist discipline had released suppressed lyric powers. Whereas, in the large motifs, realism was accentuated, there appears in the *Head* of 1932 and the *Woman Leaning on Elbows* of 1933 a sym- pls. 56, 55 bolism of form that has been freed of every possible figuration. The head could indeed be any- thing: it has something in common with a skull; it could be a mask; but the most im- portant thing about it is that the powerful outer form is lacerated or ripped open to give access to an inner space as secret as a grotto, secret and dark. In 1940 Henry Moore made a helmet and again in 1950 helmetlike heads that are his own variants of those by Lipchitz.

The *Woman Leaning on Elbows* is an even more striking example of a form in which the reality of pl. 55 the motif is forced into the background for the sake of a second expressive form. This is the creation of an arch formed by a half-shut and half-open volume. The manner in which inner space is more accessible and makes itself known to the outside strengthens the expression of a wounded world. It is, in fact, the plastic realization of a scream, a shriek, animal-like, like a lion and dark. There is even a certain savagery in the upper part with lionlike traits and a reminiscence of female breasts in the surrounding supports. The profile is different from every side, an imaginative creation in which a number of worlds seem to circulate and to evoke changes of shape. His mother's death in 1934 made a profound impression on him.

Lipchitz' creativity began to come ever more under the influence of the tensions in the world caused by the ascendancy of the Nazi party and Hitler in Germany.

It is an open question whether, from the sculptural standpoint, anything was changed because of this. The changes that had occurred till then in Lipchitz' style had been actuated by an inner necessity which, if complex, nevertheless created an inseparable unity of form and meaning. Each period had problems to solve, and each succeeding period presented different problems. The personality in which they welled up and the creativity that acted through this personality formed a constant that guaranteed the unity beneath the changes. The succession of changes did not form an evolution. The preference that certain groups of sculptors have for one or more periods of Lipchitz' work is often motivated by the evolution theory or by reasoned aesthetic or ethical considerations. But these preferences, which divide up his *œuvre*, barely conceal these sculptors' preoccupation with certain problems of their own that can be found in Lipchitz' work also and blind them to whatever is irrelevant to their own problems. Only those who can free themselves of this myopia have any chance of finding the unity that links the changes.

The '30s certainly intensified the artist's negative stance toward the destructive tendencies of the age. The positive sculpture, which was produced from the awakened memories of prehistory in the form of fabulous creatures with human traits, gave way to mythological shapes that had, not only in their titles but in their expressive content, a tangible relevance to the menacing aspects of the period. Threats to freedom found a fertile soil in Lipchitz. His Jewish youth in the tsarist empire had known the meaning of terror. The problem of what shape these feelings of terror should assume found its solution in mythological figuration. This turning to mythology was not shared by sculptors in general. Henry Moore and Barbara Hepworth continued with abstraction, although Moore rather than Hepworth was continually drawn to figuration. Both adapted the possibilities of transparent form primarily by means of tunnel-shaped grooves or holes. With Moore we notice, too, the influence of Mexican sculpture. He consciously avoids mythological motifs and concentrates on form.

Picasso learned wrought-iron procedures from Gonzales and in 1930 and 1931 came to his figurative thread plastics, of which Lipchitz' linear bronzes of 1925–26 are the precursor. Gonzales had been working in iron since 1927. He remained figurative and absorbed clear Cubist influences, and after 1929 he devoted all his attention to sculpture. From 1933 until the war his pressures changed. His linear manner of spatial creation was violent and essential; in this way he actually moved far away from figuration. On the other hand, there are works that aim at figuration in volume but even here abstract vision has its effect. Undeniably, works pl.42 such as *Head with Mirror* (1934) have certain transpositions of Lipchitz (e.g. the *Chimène* of pl.69 1930) in their immediate background. Thus, when Lipchitz made his *Barbara* in 1942, it was a continuation not of Gonzales but of himself, in the delightful *Chimène* of 1934.

Zadkine remained expressive and figurative even in his Cubist period. Moreover, in contrast with Lipchitz, not bronze but stone and wood were his source of inspiration. He chose Greek or Old Testament names for some of his sculptures: *Orpheus, Rebecca, Diana, Phoenix*. His form sometimes shocks by its disturbed quality. His reactions to current events came to light during and especially after his flight to America in 1940.

52

After his pictorial and Cubist period Laurens came to a monumental figuration in which he also attempted to revive architectonic coherence. In fact, he remained true to volume. *The Woman with the Harp* (1937) is an exception, which, unlike Lipchitz' early transparent sculptures, did not noticeably influence the modeling in his subsequent work.

When we survey the period from 1930 to 1940 the dynamic force in sculpture appears to come as much from the individual imagination as from the expression of a civilization. The tensions in the period seek their objectivization in abstraction and in reality. World events continually produced shock effects. The destructive and explosive forces of the age produced the negative effect of revulsion or protest. The collective shocks in the civilization either activated or disabled artists' creativity.

Affected both through race and through his urge for freedom by the menace of Hitlerism, Lipchitz' whole previous development now led to the cultivation of the monster, the old mystic animal. The monster appears first in the bull and the condor (1932). Lipchitz was not the only one obsessed by monsters, for the bull plays an equally important part in Picasso's work. Lipchitz found his own solution, which was, again, connected with his own temperament and experience. His creativity was never wholly free from strong primitive urges such as hunger, thirst, fear of death, and hunger for life. Did he not say that while he was busy on *Return of the Prodigal Son* he had had a strong feeling of thirst? And was he not to a large degree endowed pl. 50 with a gift of metamorphosis, known from Greek myths and loved by the Mannerists, who adored Proteus and Prometheus as themes, especially Prometheus with his ripped-out liver? Metamorphosis in forms is possible only so long as there is inward movement, an intuition that has not yet crystallized and that can be observed in the fixed form of sculpture only through the ambiguity or symbolism of the forms.

As soon as the collective tensions of the period and his own inner tensions, too, became more concrete, the strength of the metamorphosis decreased. If the *Mother and Child* (1930), the pl. 51 *Woman Leaning on Elbows* (1933), and *The Couple* (1929) still recall the young artist who, twenty pls. 55, 49 years earlier in Madrid, had gazed with such enthusiasm on the human, animal, and vegetable metamorphoses of Hieronymus Bosch, this is no longer true of Lipchitz' Prometheus series, which he began in 1936. One thinks rather of El Greco, with his exaggerated, metaphysical, and Mannerist-realist shapes. The certainty of the twisted forms exists in the flickering light of a disturbed world hurrying toward its death. Everything glows and surges; the work is executed with his earlier, relatively smooth and well-defined surfaces. One no longer knows where one surface ends and another begins, so that the edges are no longer lines but flickering lights on the high points of the swollen surface. An El Greco-like light flashes like lightning over the shapes, which quiver in their excess tension and are seized by horror of the labyrinth. Figures regain hands and feet; faces become full, as if order deliberately wanted to set itself up in opposition to the whirlwind of an assaulting disorder. Realism does not return quietly and assured, like a prodigal son from the world of the sins of abstraction; instead, a realism that has become alarmed and vibrates in an invisible current of eddying forces announces itself.

Some have wanted to term this style Baroque. Several times Mannerist rather than Baroque elements have been noted in modern art, including Lipchitz' sculpture, without our being able to call the complex of art after 1900 Mannerist in its entirety. At any rate, the expressive, deforming, and abstract side of art is so closely linked with positive inward drives in the artists that one can speak of their collective reaction to their time. A group of men of genius has given the half century its appearance of endless turbulence.

fig.LIX,pl.62   From 1933 to 1939 mythological-struggle themes developed, to which the Prometheus series,
figs.LX,LXI   the *Rape of Europa*, and the Theseus theme, executed later in America, all belong. Paralleling this development the earlier themes continued, among them the mother-and-child motif in a new and very important phase.

After his mother's death in 1934, Lipchitz went back to Russia to visit a sister. As Alfred Barr and Henry Hope have established, and Lipchitz confirmed to me with the addition of a detail, on his way home from the theater one rainy night he heard a woman singing. A creature without legs was propelling herself along in a little cart, singing with upraised arms, her hair soaked through and hanging down her back. The scene made a deep impression on him. He forgot it—until in 1939 he produced a gouache on the mother-and-child theme. The child hangs on to the mutilated woman and is dependent on her. In the earliest mother-and-
pl.19   child treatment (1914–15) the child does not hang but sits and is carried; in the already tragic
pl.51   birdlike motif (1930) the child hangs on her back and is carried by the groaning, kneeling
pls.64,65,66   mother. In the 1939 version, which grew in 1941–45 into the touching image of the cripple,

54

the child clings to her helplessly. Only then did the sculptor remember the crowded-out scene of the rainy night in Russia, and only then did he discover how the torso had come through the vigor of the metamorphosis to appear like the head of a bull.

The demonic monster was mixed with the mother image. The bull became the symbol through which he projected his fear of the collapse of Europe. The beginning was simpler. He was to make a sculpture for the International Exhibition in Paris in 1937 to adorn one of the entrances of a room in the Grand Palais dedicated to Science. Lipchitz thought of the son of the Titan who stole fire for mankind, Prometheus, the creator of men out of clay and water. In 1936–37 he produced a first sketch for Prometheus. The oppressive atmosphere in Europe gave Lipchitz pl.8 the idea of designing the free Prometheus, wrestling with the vulture of Zeus. Lipchitz does not keep to the myth, which allows Heracles to kill the vulture and free Prometheus. Prometheus himself struggles with the vulture and strangles it—so, at least, in the myth as Lipchitz changed it to his own liking. The figure was gigantic. It was conceived on the superman scale of the Greek gods. The two struggling figures are again a unity, but through combat, not fig.LX love. The gouache and the first sketch for the *Rape of Europa* are similar in form. This group is pls.59,60 even more complex. Lipchitz also produced horizontal versions.

The significance of Prometheus' struggle with the vulture was clearly grasped in the extremely tense political atmosphere of France. A press campaign against Lipchitz left no one in any doubt about the feelings of certain circles with respect to his viewpoint. An artist had shown that myth, too, could be revived in the twentieth century as reality and not only as a figment of the imagination.

The form of these sculptures was positive and laid emphasis on volume. Disturbed by a mighty unrest, the volume is composed like a stream of rises and declines, so increasing its dramatic character. The mature experience of the sculptor's Cubist and transparent periods had its effect. Thus technical considerations caused changes in the position and actions of the hands in successive drafts.

For the second time Lipchitz had to face a momentous personal decision—whether to depart from the land and the civilization of his beloved France, where he had grown as a sculptor. After the German invasion of France, knowing the adverse opinion held of him by the German and French Nazis, he and his wife had to flee the house and atelier in Boulogne-sur-Seine, leaving the contents behind. Separated, after an interval with work in Toulouse, from everything in France that had encouraged his work and urged to come by the Museum of Modern Art, he attempted to resume life in America. After a miserable boat journey from Portugal, he began life anew in June, 1941. His only possessions were two statuettes, a portfolio with drawings, and a few dollars.

It could have been the conclusion to a fruitful past, but it was this only in part. In New York his circumstances changed but not at once for the better. Eventually he was able to live at Washington Square South in the artists' quarter. Among other offers was that of a post as professor of sculpture. He turned all offers down, because for him only one thing existed: the chance to discover how and where his sculpture could start afresh. For this he sacrificed more immediate advantages and had to endure an intensely difficult period of wretched lodgings and slender income. Kurt Valentin, who had an exceptionally good art business and had specialized in sculpture—which was rare, even in Europe—then offered him the assistance that brought him back into activity. The difficulties were great, but he persisted with the unshakable strength of a creator.

At first his work did not change, so little was it dependent in the beginning upon his altered surroundings. The themes that welled up in him from his cultural and creative vulnerability had already been sown in France and had taken root. Everything had remained in him. For some time before the war broke out, a brake had been put on his sculpture. He had made many sketches. He never ceased to make sketches, even during the work; it was an incessant need of his active spirit and hands; he was like a violinist who can leave none of his fingers without practice. Like Van Gogh, his mode of expression had to be as rapid and direct as possible. Therefore, though he could carve in stone and wood, he finally let modeling dominate, but it was modeling based on a vast knowledge of bronzecasting. Drawing was even faster, but here color was the great temptation. He made trials with color on reliefs to find out what color could bring about in spatial effects. His drawing style altered with the style of his sculptures. The drawings always bore some relation to sculpture and were conceived sculpturally. Likewise, the color of his spatial drawings had spatial significance. He knew what temptations awaited him in color. The Greeks, he said, painted their statuary to reduce the excessive effects of strong light on light marble and produce quieter effects. After the polychrome reliefs

XLVII   The Meeting, *1913*
XLVIII   The Couple, *1929*
IL   The Embrace, *1934*
L   Song of Songs, *1946*

XLVII

XLVIII

IL

L

LI

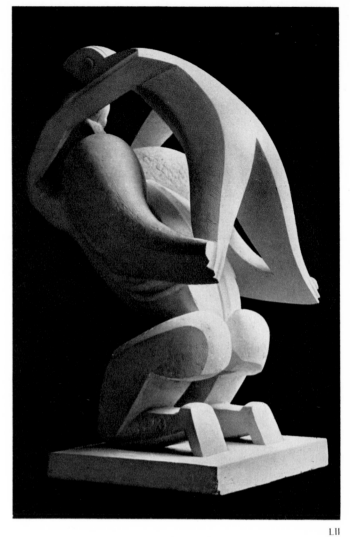

LII

LIII

B. Mother and Child

LIV

LV

LVI

LVII

C. Mythical Combatants

LVIII *Study for* "David and Goliath", *1930*
LIX Prometheus and the Vulture, *1936*
LX Rape of Europa, *1938*
LXI Theseus, *1942*

LVIII

LIX

LX

LXI

he limited his use of color as much as possible in order not to be sidetracked, and he avoided the dangers of pictorial sculpture.

The drawings that he was able to take with him on his flight were, along with two small sculptures, expressions of what obsessed him—departure and arrival. The child appears again in the later motif. Again two worlds are involved in it. The child is his sculpture and the child is what he has dreamed. He rescues the child in himself. And, as always in the last years, the personal element is linked with the fate of France and of the world. The tragic sculpture already mentioned, of the crippled mother with the clinging, dependent child, was produced in New York.

The power of metamorphosis reappeared, but the form is somewhat less passionately swollen. The monster dwelt in the woman's torso.

Lipchitz was able to continue the Prometheus series through a commission from the Ministry of Education and Health in Rio de Janeiro. In 1936 a group of architects led by Le Corbusier had begun plans for vast new office blocks and government buildings. Lipchitz designed a Prometheus for the Ministry, the theme of which is provided by a panel with a strongly pl.61 waving horizontal center line. The figure with the vulture creates the impression of an approaching thunderstorm. The heavy sculpture is so balanced that its mass can be supported on the minimal round form, the lowest point of the panel. By accident it was executed on much too small a scale, so that the conception did not achieve its plastic effect on a large, separate expanse of wall. For the Philadelphia Museum, Lipchitz was able to execute it in its correct pl.63 dimensions. Seeing it there on the staircase one cannot help marveling that so great a volume seems so weightless and yet expresses an almost irresistible turbulence that is controlled and held in balance down to the smallest detail. It is as if all his previous experience with the transparent forms and the later voluminous forms had combined to create this composition based exclusively upon rounded forms.

In actuality he felt himself freed of the Parisian past. He was not attached to all that he had left behind. On the contrary, in some ways he could breathe more freely. Less than ever now did he subject himself to any one achieved form. The years 1941 to 1943 show an inconceivably rich, many-sided production. As the transparent forms had broken free in 1925–26 with lyric energy after the pressure of Cubism, so now the transparent forms broke free

again after the tensions of France. There is a difference, however. There appear—simultane-
figs.LI–LV, ously with the mother-and-child projects, the Prometheus and Theseus motifs, and the bene-
LXI–LIX dictions—prayers for the fate of France in a severe, almost Arp-like round form with round
pls.77,78 openings, more abstract than the Prometheus and the Mother and Child, as if their gestures had
needed restraining and clarification.

The new transparent forms are full of erotic and symbolic imagery, rich in linear expression,
sometimes playful, sometimes grotesque, or with a heavier, more ritualistic emphasis. The
three worlds of plant, animal, and man flow into one another with a naturalness explicable only
by the direct, unhindered working of the artist's creative powers.

Bronzes are among the strongest work, being somewhat heavier in mass and without the
pl.74 tenuous, enchanting upward motion of *The Promise* (1942) and its associated works, *The Fiancé*,
pls.67,68 the two versions of *Yara*, and the *Innocent Victim*. *Spring* (1942) and *Blossoming* (1941–42) are
reminiscent of old Asiatic bronzes, ritual sacrificial pots and bowls from the Chou and Han
dynasties. Flower, fruit, plant, and woman unite into one shape. Erotic imagery and age-old
fertility symbolism give the sculpture an enduring quality.

The primary drive behind the production of these years was sacrifice. The feeling of release and
safety was not unqualified. In the Cubist period also, with its severe verticality, it was clear
that a magic world was inhabited by the unconscious memories of ancient ritual in the depths
of the sculptor's unconscious. His creativity was attracted not only to the Hebrew world,
which was familiar to him from family tradition, but also by the ritual actions and shapes
of Mediterranean civilization. Fear of the invisible god and the desire to point out the menacing
features of the age and to know the future were not wholly alien to the sometimes prophetic
power with which sculptural visions were formed within him. Especially in the years 1942
and 1943 the idea of sacrifice had its effect. The Mannerism of the form increased almost to
pls.75,76 excess. The terrible sight of opened intestines *(The Pilgrim, Prayer)*, familiar from twentieth century Surrealism and from the ritual prophecies of divine will—from intestines and
other omens in Mesopotamia and Etruria—was surpassed by the remarkable conception of the
pl.73 statue *Myrah* that reveals in the arabesques of an exotic shell the scheme of a pelvis freed of its
intestines. It is not impossible that the different rhythms of his American surroundings were
having their effect upon him and that his separation from France and his torment at the fate of

62

the Jews brought about extremely complex tensions that demanded release. The ecstatic, vibrating, and lacerated character of the form is the immediate expression of a wounded world, the mutilated world which, like Job, cries out its sorrow to the Lord.

Two commissions, that already mentioned for *Prometheus* and a *Pegasus* for a new museum, pl.61 kept Lipchitz busy from 1944 until he returned for a while to liberated France in 1946. The Galerie Maeght held an exhibition of his work, where he and his work were greeted with joyful acclaim. In his Boulogne-sur-Seine atelier, originally left untenanted and later taken over by the painter Pignon, he gradually reassembled what was left of his old work. It was good to be back. The great pioneer of the revival of sacred art in Catholic churches, Père Couturier, saw his work at Maeght's and, sensing intuitively its religious basis, managed to get him a commission for a baptismal font for the church of Notre-Dame-de-Toute-Grâce at pl.89 Assy in the Haute-Savoie, on the sculptor's condition, which was accepted, that he might set in some visible place the following inscription: *Jacob Lipchitz juif fidèle à la foi de ses ancêtres a fait cette Vierge pour la bonne entente des hommes sur la terre afin que l'esprit règne.* (Jacob Lipchitz, of Jewish extraction, and true to the faith of his ancestors, made this Virgin, to further good-will among men so that the spirit may triumph on earth.)

But Paris and France could no longer keep him. With mixed feelings at seeing the past and his scattered belongings coming back to him, he began to feel that the past was going to seize him. After much inner conflict, distraught by personal problems, he decided to settle in America. Nearly all the others, Zadkine, Léger, Chagall, and Ernst, had sought out again the familiar and vibrant Paris milieu whose people and atmosphere seemed indispensable for their artistic well-being. Lipchitz seemed a match for the other hard and tensed American way of life. He no longer needed the diversions of Paris and access to his fellow artists so much. He scarcely did any traveling. Moreover, he got on well with a number of Americans who loved art with a rare and often unspoiled enthusiasm. Their enterprise and verve attracted him, and he was fond above all of the magnificent natural scenery close to New York. He moved to Hastings-on-Hudson, where he felt content among the rocks not far from the broad, powerful river, in rural surroundings and yet with New York close at hand. His first wife Berthe Kitrosser remained in Boulogne, and Lipchitz married Yulla Halberstadt.

At first the image of *Notre Dame de Liesse* (Our lady of Joy) would not come. She suddenly pl.89

appeared to him during a ride on the New York subway. After that he found no more peace. He produced scribbles, and in a spate of energy he began finally in 1948 on the great commission. Meanwhile one of his heart's desires was fulfilled in the birth of his daughter Lolya Rachel. Now for the first time he produced motifs that have a conscious relation to the child, the mother, and himself.

The designs for *Notre Dame de Liesse* changed. He managed to have the project modified so that it no longer needed to be a font. The sculpture was to stand in the choir. Someting of the pl.68,fig.XLIII bronze *Spring*, *Blossoming*, *The Cradle*, not forgetting the rising *Yara*, comes into the basic form, which ultimately rests on the Lamb and the three archangels. But it took a long time before he got so far. The relations between the open heart, framed by the three parts of heaven and held together by the dove, and the supporting member, changed continually. The transparent inner space enclosed the Virgin, whose shape cuts off the fourth side.

During this period, in January, 1952, his atelier at 2 East 23rd Street near Madison Square, which he had had ever since 1942, burnt down. Much of his work and many documents were lost. This was a great blow to the sculptor, who saw more than ten years of his work damaged or destroyed, including the most advanced designs for Assy. With the help of individuals and museums he was able to build a large new atelier right by the Hudson and not far from his home, so that he could execute larger commissions there. His brother, who tirelessly protected his interests, sent him the remaining pieces from Paris to New York to help tide him over the emptiness of the gutted atelier. Lipchitz himself found the strength to say that the fire was perhaps a punishment for his not yet making the Madonna beautiful enough and for deviating too much from her first appearance to him. He had the chance now to do her better. His imagination saw Mary in flames, and, hence, a new design was produced with tongues of flame licking around her, like a bronze Buddha. Later they disappeared again. On the reverse side of pl.89 the sculpture he placed the inscription with the Beethoven-like sound, (p. 63). The sculpture of Mary had led by a remarkable detour once more to the founding of a chapel on a large site specially built for *Notre Dame de Liesse*. The sculpture was given a setting and in the vicinity the chapel was surrounded by an enclosure for which Lipchitz designed the trelliswork. Philip Johnson, architectural associate of Mies van der Rohe, designed the building during the years 1957–58.

64

Once again, it seems as if the large commissions for a time wholly absorbed all Lipchitz' imaginative and creative energies and then left certain sides of him unsatisfied.

The inextinguishable gift of metamorphosis persisted in him without being able to express itself adequately. How else is one to explain why, when he was busy with the *Notre Dame de Liesse*, he should suddenly notice a chisel that had lost its handle lying on his studio floor, and see a little man in it? He added something to it: he combined two elements, then four, and, playing with it with all his technical ingenuity and invention, he produced in amusement a series of witty variations on the theme, much as a composer may modify a theme that he, or someone else, has written. pls.91,92, 93,94,95

Whoever wants to approach Lipchitz in the inconceivable number of facets that his creativity contains should think of the large pieces of work that were produced simultaneously or in quick succession, informed by the lyricism of the transparent forms, the chisel variations, or the "semi-automatics." The same need to revive certain forces arose through the year-long pressures of his exacting activity on the *Man with the Eagle*, finished only in 1958, which had been commissioned for Fairmount Park, Philadelphia, as an allegory of initiative. pl.100

He sought to portray solace in the thirty-three semi-automatic expressions of 1955–56. He literally intended them as explosions after the *Virgin* and the twelve-foot-high *Man with the Eagle*. Possibly a semi-automatic element had existed in the transparent forms of 1925. The expression of thirty years later, however, is even more clearly based on the revival of tactile interest. Lipchitz once termed sculpture "le soleil à la portée de la main." Commenting on this later, he said: "Not only the way that sculpture radiates warmth, life, and light is comprehended in the symbol of the sun, but also sculpture's cosmic element." It is typical of Lipchitz that he could not leave it at the more or less literal utterance. "A la portée de la main" was necessary because he wanted in this way to realize the tangibility of sculpture. pl.89

He began blindly, by forming a mass of clay or plasticine under water. He started from whatever his hands presented to him, without any optical control. Unlike the blind, Lipchitz has a conception of space formed by seeing and touching. This experience naturally also persists in him unconsciously and cannot be eliminated. After the automatic preliminaries he corrected only the form that, from his technical knowledge of bronzecasting, appeared to him predominant, and then continued to work at it and develop it. Hence the name "semi-automatic."

Sometimes his mood changed from one day to the next, and then he altered something, without, however, affecting the original form. This birth in a shape without name and apparently free is unusually attractive, but in reality it is bound to certain types of images that are apparently submerged in the unconscious as primary forms and limited in number. Their flowing character and the motifs often appear linked with what we find previously in his conscious and pl.99 controlled production. One of the most beautiful, with a distant recollection of the *Victory of Samothrace*, is in remembrance of the dancer Loie Fuller.

He regarded the series as an intermezzo, nothing to be persevered in. These moments in a long existence as sculptor are actual openings, chinks in the hermetic creative process that the Surrealists wanted for several years to lay bare. Lipchitz' utterances recall in another respect what had happened when Paul Klee in 1914 made his short but very important trip to Tunis in North Africa. Klee said then that drawing, as the expressive movement of the hand, is in principle so different from the use of tone and color, that one could effect graphic expression very well even in the darkest night. He, too, had hit on the idea, though only for the graphic arts, of withdrawing from the light and trusting to the expressive movements of the hand. He did not yet speak of "automatic."*

In the same context he remarks that "creation lives like Genesis beneath the visible surface of the work. All intellectuals see this with respect to the past but only the creative minds see it also with respect to the future."** These meditations which, for all their brevity, strike deep, touch in their essential what Lipchitz under other circumstances had experienced with respect to the three-dimensional. He had taken the skin off his sculpture. It lay bare and open. In a dark pre-existence he permits the groping hands to have their full sway.

figs.LVI,LVII Meanwhile the mother-and-child motif had taken on a mythological shape in the Hagar studies pls.86,87 and the sculpture that occupied him from 1948 onward. In the Old Testament account the Egyptian Hagar was renounced by Abraham. In the desert, alone with the thirsty child and without water, she feared that the child would perish; in her despair, she heard the divine, angelic voice that roused her to trust and hope; and in a vision she is shown the spring where she can find refreshment. From this conflict of feelings, which once again had its roots in his own

* Diary page 928.
** Diary page 932.

66

recent experience of life and marriage and conscience, a gesture arose in his sculpture of a raised hand terminating a rising, undulating movement. The motif gave him no peace. The motif awakes metaphysical thirst in him—the great thirst for refreshment that trust brings. There was the recumbent Hagar protecting and concealing the child in her lap. An element of pathos indicated that Lipchitz was personally affected. This expressed itself ecstatically in the same year in the miracle sculptures—the prayers said aloud in a passionate gesture opposite the seven miraculous candles, which are split and distorted and raise themselves like the flaming hand. El Greco comes back into the plastic arts. In all this movement one thinks literally of the central figure of the *Notre Dame de Liesse*, in which everything that had given the artist human pain converges, struggles, and continually re-arises. The symmetry that we saw in his beginnings in 1913 now returned, angular and severe, although now everything flowed. In the Virgin there is a rising and falling movement that converges in the symbol of the Holy Ghost.

Thus in half a century an *œuvre* had come into being, fierce, taut, begun with concentration and closure. The author had staked on it everything that he had in him. After the beginning the inner tensions relaxed and the sculpture shifted from inorganic and geometric images to organic.

Motifs of birth, life, and death grew in him and shocked him. He discovered darkness, the void, and the cleft, using them to create happiness in a complex rhythm—one pattern with its own logic for the three empires of plant, animal, and man—one pattern in which man alone is not the criterion. Metamorphosis came to dominate his work. The pressure of the age made the tensions more concrete. Symbols grew. Themes of struggle were presented mythologically but were experienced intensely as present-day reality. Humanity gained a more passionate gesture, a tragic rhythm. Lipchitz' creativity never became static, made no fixed contracts either with Cubism or with the transparent forms, or with symbolic expressive realism. A sovereign, ever-present, invisible, incomprehensible power directed and maintained everything and manifested itself in a hundred different forms.

Only in Rodin's *œuvre*, in the nineteenth century, are we aware of a similar, though less varied, almost superhuman creative energy. Lipchitz is inextricably in the grip of that cosmic designing power. The significance of his *œuvre*, not yet concluded and already of influence everywhere, cannot yet be finally estimated. The man who spoke of the royal road of art through the centuries and of the great current has already opened up to us a view of that road and has made us feel the force of that current. Now we have a true epic, an Odyssey in the empire of sculpture.

Portion of a letter from Lipchitz to the author, April 25, 1958

l'image de ma mère. Je n'y peux rien, l'artiste ne peut pas se rendre compte de tous les aspects de ce que sort de lui et c'est tant mieux, je pense. Avec "Figure" je me souviens nettement que mes préoccupations étaient surtout d'ordre constructive, évidemment, il y a tout à coup ces yeux fascinants et ce semblant de sexe, alors..... mais consciemment je peux dire que je n'y suis pour rien.

En effet, à présent que vous me signalez la similitude entre la statue de 1916 et "Figure", je la vois aussi, mais jamais je n'y ai pensé auparavant. Cela vient probablement de mon inclination de travailler avec des éléments tirés de la nature. C'est là mon "raw material" et c'est probablement ça qui sert de trait d'union entre tout ce que je fais.

L'incendie du musée m'a rendu malade, heureusement les dégas ne sont pas énormes en comparaison de ce que cela pouvait être Dieu soit loué !

Comment se présente l'Exposition de Bruxelles ?

Avec mes hommages respectueux pour Madame Hammacher, croyez moi, mon cher Directeur, votre bien dévoué

Lipchitz

Lipchitz' reflections on art

Instead of expressing thoughts about art, I shall confide in you.

One thing dulled my joy in work when I was first beginning: an opinion – that famous opinion of Leonardo da Vinci concerning sculptors and sculpture. You are familiar with it, aren't you?

It forcefully impressed on me how matter holds us in bondage, how impossible it was for our hands to follow the palpitations of our hearts and the mad course of our imaginations.

I was unhappy about it until the day when Providence revealed to me those "light, airy, and transparent things that can be seen, and can move us from all sides at once."

From then on, I could soar with this "heavier than air," which is sculpture

Oh! If only the shade of Leonardo could modify his judgment!

Roger Vitrac: Jacques Lipchitz (Les sculpteurs français nouveaux, 7). Paris, Librairie Gallimard, 1929

Questionnaire

1 What should you most like to do, to know, to be? (In case you are not satisfied).
2 Why wouldn't you change places with any other human being?
3 What do you look forward to?
4 What do you fear most from the future?
5 What has been the happiest moment of your life? The unhappiest? (If you care to tell).
6 What do you consider your weakest characteristics? Your strongest? What do you like most about yourself? Dislike most?
7 What things do you really like? Dislike? (Nature, people, ideas, objects, etc. Answer in a phrase or a page, as you will).
8 What is your attitude toward art today?
9 What is your world view? (Are you a reasonable being in a reasonable scheme?)
10 Why do you go on living?

It's almost a confession you're asking

Here are my answers in the order of your questions.
1 For me to do is to be and the possibility of knowing.
2 But quite simply because I am incapable of being anything but what I am.
3 I don't think of the future. Only the present concerns me.
4 I repeat – the future doesn't concern me.

5 Probably the happiest moment is the moment I was born. It seems I smiled.
   As to the unhappy moments they're too long to relate.
6 Ah, if only I could know that, but I think I am like everybody else weak and strong,
   cowardly and brave, good and bad, and really there's no cause to be satisfied with oneself.
7 I have a formidable appetite. I really like many things.
8 The question is too vast – all that is being done in our time is "the art of today".
   I myself like only a certain art which gives me the illusion that we are not altogether
   abject animals and which gives us the hope of some day becoming men.
9 I am a Jew and I carry in my veins the revelation of unity.
10 I have told you already: I have a ferocious appetite and a curiosity without bounds.

The Little Review, May, 1929

In 1918, almost at the end of World War I, I left my Paris studio to work in the country. I went to Beaulieu pres Loches and immediately I encountered great problems. It was absolutely impossible to continue the same work I had been doing in Paris because of material difficulties.

So I decided to carve a few bas-reliefs directly in stone. At that time I was preoccupied with the idea of polychromed sculpture – which means for me not just to colour a carved surface but to conceive a sculptured form in colour from the beginning. I found two plaques of stone and made two bas-reliefs, one multicoloured and the other one in different shades of one colour to white. I made before preliminary studies in gouache and somehow liked them. And since I had to bring my production once a month to my Paris dealer and realized that it was no easy task to travel during the war with a stone, I decided to make only studies in casein or gouache to be carved later after the return to my studio.

As it happened, this plan to carve them later never materialized because I became interested in other work. Here you see a few of these studies made in Beaulieu and also some earlier studies for sculpture. Only the number 17 was made after I carved the bas-relief in stone to find out how to enrich some forms with colour. I add to this little exhibit two polychromed stones to shed some light on the significance of these studies. One of the two stones was made in Beaulieu and the other one later in 1921 in Paris in the same spirit.

Hastings-on-Hudson, September, 1955   Jacques Lipchitz

Jacques Lipchitz: Studies for Polychromed Bas-Reliefs, Cubist Drawings, and Gouaches, 1912–1919.
Catalogue of exhibiton held September 26–October 8, 1955 at the New Gallery, New York

On Rodin

In my youth, as long as I thought that Rodin – like the other sculptors – made only statues, I preferred some of the others to him because their work seemed to me more harmonious. Until one day I understood that it was not beauty – not just the external beauty of the forms – he was looking for; I understood he was trying to realize *The Gate of Hell*.

At this moment everything became clear to me. And from then on, having the possibility of entering freely into one of the most majestic human edifices, I discovered there all the treasures and all the riches piled-up in great profusion. And "piled-up" is the right word for it: all the technical innovations, all liberties, all audacities, all the intuitions; in short, all the elements of an art in the making were there. Cézanne and Maillol, Matisse and Brancusi; even the Surrealists with their automatic writing and double images; and something more – an immense creation: *The Gate of Hell*.

To me there is no difference between painting and sculpture; they are like two different musical instruments. For instance, a violin and a piano. Naturally each has a different sonority, and different techniques are required to master them. But the important thing is the music they produce.

At this point I cannot refrain from asking a question which is born from the affirmations of so many critics and of so many art historians who have been saying that sculpture is following the innovations of the painters: "Is it really sculpture which is following painting?"

Here we have Rodin to contradict this opinion. At the same time that the sculptor Rodin was creating *The Gate of Hell*, a painter, Maurice Denis, who could be considered the mouthpiece of his fellow painters, wrote in his book *Theories*: "*One must remember that a painting before being a warhorse, a female nude or some sort of anecdote, is essentially a flat surface covered with colors that are assembled in a certain order.*" (The same ideas may be applied to sculpture, and we can see today to what kind of a dead end these ideas are leading us.)

Among the artists at that time, only Cézanne and Rodin used the elements found in nature to raise a work of art so as to become a symbol. Isn't it astonishing that Emile Zola, with remarkable intuition, selected Cézanne and Rodin from the many artists living at this time to be used as prototypes for the heroes Lantier and Mahoudeau in his novel *L'Œuvre* written in 1885? Miraculous indeed! Nevertheless an art editor, enriched by dealing with the Impressionists, dared to ridicule Zola as an art connoisseur in a book he wrote on Cézanne. Or this: a truly honest man in a recent book of memoirs tries to belittle Rodin because he courted a Duchess and wore gloves *beurre frais!*

But all these authors achieve is the lowering of their own spiritual level. Let us forget about them.

The names of Cézanne and Rodin will live forever in the glory of the eternal light as the two geniuses to whom we owe our completely renewed vision.   *Translated from the French*

Hastings-on-Hudson, 1954.   *Auguste Rodin*. Catalogue of exhibition held May 4–29, 1954
                                             at the Curt Valentin Gallery, New York

Dear Otto,

You asked me to write a few words of introduction for your coming exhibition of sculpture. I do so with great pleasure.

Looking over the list of exhibitors, I notice that besides the giants of the past century you also give a place to some names of the present generation. For this generosity let me thank you. You are perfectly right. Life continues, and so does sculpture.

Often sculpture was defined as "volumes in space"; I always found this definition very poor. More than thirty years ago I was asked by the directors of *Esprit Nouveau* to write an article about sculpture. I remember that I finished, maybe a little pompously, with the sentence: "La sculpture c'est du Soleil à la portée de la main". (Sculpture is a Sun which can be reached by hand). I had my reasons for saying that: First, because of the warmth, life and light which sculpture radiates; and second, by "à la portée de la main", I wanted to show the touchability of sculpture. And I called upon the Sun to show the cosmic quality of sculpture.

Indeed, sculpture is a man-made companion with an immortal human heart inside from which calls are emitted constantly giving us joy, warming us and teaching us, all at the same time.

You know that I am a mad collector. While writing, I am sitting here in my room surrounded by millenniums of sculptures from all over the globe. They are all speaking to me, I try to understand them, and I never feel alone.

[signed] J. Lipchitz

Sculpture 1880–1957. Catalogue of exhibition held December 10, 1957–January 11, 1958 at the Fine Arts Associates, New York

I call them Semi-Automatics because these sculptures originate completely automatically in the blind. The form which I obtain in this way is first of all examined by me from a technical point of view. Everything I judge too fragile or not suitable for the bronze is taken away.

By manipulating my form in such a manner, a lot of images suggest themselves to my attention. Ordinarily, one image is predominant.

This one I choose.

And from that point on, I continue consciously until the vision I had becomes clarified.

Sometimes, from one day to the next my vision changes because my mood has changed. And then the sculpture is modified – not the original form – to suit my new inspiration. It is fascinating for me to observe these modifications over which I have no control.

During the almost half-century I have been a sculptor, I remark that after periods of tense and controlled work I feel a strong urge for a kind of free lyrical expansion that cannot be stopped. So came my "transparents" in 1925 after a long period of hard fight for a new language. So came in 1942 my "transparents" here in this country after the tense years of war and my flight from Paris. So came my "variations on a chisel" after the fire in my studio in 1952. And now after a few years of working on my "Virgin" and the sculture for the Fairmont [*sic*] Park, I literally exploded into these semi-automatics. I do not intend to turn this process into a durable way of working. I hope with these thirty-three semi-automatics my obsession will have come to an end having enriched my imagination with more freedom. I would like to add: I did not make any choice among my forms; I faced them all.

I found it interesting to confront with these semi-automatics a choice of my sculptures made between 1915–1928, so self-restrained, so precise, to show that by and by it retracts, by and by it expands, but it is always the same heart that beats.

Hastings-on-Hudson, *1957*   Jacques Lipchitz

Jacques Lipchitz: Thirty-Three Semi-Automatics, 1955-1956 and Earlier Works, 1915–1928. Catalogue of exhibition held March 5–30, 1957 at the Fine Arts Associates, New York

Conversation with Lipchitz

Excerpts of a conversation between Lipchitz and art critic Cranston Jones, November 1957

Lipchitz: ...I didn't like Rodin at that time. I liked, oddly, the Greek – you know, the very Olympian art. I, as a young boy, absolutely raw, couldn't understand Rodin, whose work was the last, the highest mathematics of the time – you know, the highest form. And I couldn't understand Gauguin. I remember, a friend of mine brought me to Vollard, the art dealer in Rue Laffitte, and I looked at a painting by Gauguin – "The Fight of the Angel with Jacob." And I swear that I couldn't see what it represented. I was so raw – I didn't see any image. And I saw, lately, this painting, and I was astonished. How could I have been so blind not to see it. Well, when I saw that painting the first time, immediately, I realized that I am very raw, and I had to bind myself – to link myself to the entire human civilization in art. I was going every day to a museum, and not only with my eyes – I was drawing. I had little money; so I was taking a sandwich of some type – even a raw onion. You know, I think that all those Venuses and Apollos had never smelled as much onion before my time. I was drawing and, also, I was collecting. I remember, for example, that in a little bric-à-brac shop behind the Châtelet in Paris, I was attracted by a painted wooden statuette. I thought it was Egyptian. Later I discovered it wasn't. But I bought it. To buy it, I didn't eat my dinner during a few days. Otherwise I couldn't have bought it. And only a year and a half later, when I came, once, to see the museum of Trocadéro, I saw that it was a Negro piece from the Dahomey tribe. I still have it....

74

Lipchitz : The man – the man – all the men from all the ages, from all time, from all the globe are with me. And I see that they are similar to me. I have that measure. Then from that I can confirm or try to go ahead to break this measure or to find some new path. That's what is my attitude. It gives me strength. You see, I don't approach things aesthetically. It's not only the aesthetic part which interests me. It's the man who did it – what he felt. And he speaks to me through this language of sculpture; and I try to understand him. And then he gives me the measure of the human being. You see, now we are living in a very interesting epoch – very extraordinary – because we discovered the entire globe; and we discovered what is done everywhere around the globe. And now the need of our art is that we must look for a universal language. You know, we observe so much that we cannot digest easily what we observe....

Lipchitz :... I'm going from nature to a kind of crystal, from organic life to some kind of nonorganic life. So at that time, when I came to this period, I felt a danger. I felt a soul was going away from me. I thought that I was becoming crazy. I made articles which I destroyed at that time because I was afraid of them. I said My Lord, that's absolutely crazy. It was more than forty years ago.

So I stopped a little bit. I started to draw after nature and to meditate. I decided to take the reverse road to go from nonorganic forms to organic forms – towards life....

Jones : You often seem to see art as a kind of struggle. What do you feel are the responsibilities of the artist in this combat?

Lipchitz :... It's quite a question – quite a question. It's very difficult to explain. But when I am working I feel related to the entire cosmos. By the rhythm of my work I am related to time; by the volume of space I am related to space; by the subject matter I'm related to the human being with all his sufferings and all his joys....

Lipchitz :... You see, I'm now for almost fifty years a professional sculptor – half a century. And I always was asking myself: what is art? It's such a powerful drive. What makes me drive? What gives me the impulse to make art? And I found out. I don't know if it is the real answer. But for me it is the real answer. It's a kind of desire to fight against death. Love is that, too. But art is a human way. Procreation – the animals have procreation, and they are driven by this powerful thing which pushes them to make the species survive. But human beings have art and that differentiates them from the animal. And there comes a time when you feel this continuity, this immortality of art. At that time you find... our Lord.

Presented on NCB-TV March 9, 1958 as part of the series *Wisdom: Conversations with the Elder Wise Men of Our Day*. (Copyright © 1958 by National Broadcasting Company, Inc.)

Excerpts from reactions to Lipchitz' work

between 1917 and 1958

1 Max Jacob's inscription to Lipchitz in Jacob's book *La Côte-Recueil de chants celtiques*. Paul Birault, Paris, 1911.
"Art is not very rich in sculpture. Indeed, my dear Lipsiche [*sic*], it is said that when one comes to you quality is everything. Max Jacob, 3 February, 1917, 17, Rue Galvielle, Paris 17e."

2 André Salmon, 1920, in connection with Lipchitz' work exhibited at the Salon des Indépendents, in *L'Europe Nouvelle*, Feb. 1920.
"Exploring his secret further and more deeply than anyone else, with theoretical works which one might place beside those in carved wood which Brancusi exhibits in 1920, Lipchitz has not ceased for a moment to hope for a return into those regions which, though still spiritual, are already terrestrial, where man arranges numbers on the one plane where they do not confound him....
"Among the Cubists, who were above all painters and graphic artists, Jacques Lipchitz is one of the very few sculptors and he is already in a position to influence the sculpture of this school. He might even provide an artist such as Laurens, whom one sees forced to reject the strait-jacket of the system, with the means of salvation without restricting Laurens' very lively personality....
"I can imagine the modern Temple (I mean a building buzzing with fruitful activity, open for the worship of public art) that a collaboration between Jacques Lipchitz and the architect Duchamp-Villon might have given us!"

3 Waldemar George, in *L'Amour de l'Art*. August 1921.
"Jacques Lipchitz, scarcely 20 years of age, made a series of busts that testify to his perfect mastery and profound knowledge of the sculptor's craft. His surface modeling constitutes a mode of plastic expression and remains strictly subordinated to the organic laws of the work.
"...Whereas the essential principles of the Cubist school, namely, the dissociation of color and form, the interpenetration of planes, etc., were present in his earliest bas-reliefs, Jacques Lipchitz nowadays conceives work that is at once simpler and more intellectual, conserving only an almost imperceptible trace of the natural element whose shape it evokes."

4 Jean Cocteau who posed as a model for Lipchitz, in *Broom*, June 1922. This report was translated from the French and published only in English.
"The cold hypnotized me and gave me the strange feeling of surgical operations. Thus I found myself rigid and without strength, ready to submit to the experiment. The problem was to combine light and shade in my likeness, not by copying my face and then simplifying it, nor by deforming it afterwards on the pretext of style.
"...a fresh problem presents itself to Lipchitz the portraitist, since he never does things by halves. Neither the cast, the stylization nor the monstrousness. What remains? A hunt for light more difficult than writing different sentences with the right and left hand. A terrible hunt with all kinds of small arms, silences, unheard of halts. The two quarries draw near; light first. It lies down and allows itself to be caressed. After comes the likeness.
"The capture of likeness was a very long affair. Brusquely, like the effect of a drug on the organism, it came from all sides. It was captured and the day in which the two savage beasts understood each other to perfection and became domestic animals, Lipchitz decapitated me."

5 [Anonymous] "The Technique of Jacques Lipchitz," in *Broom*, June 1922.
"At the beginning of his career Jacques Lipchitz executed works which were distinguished by their artistic maturity. With rapid strides he advanced towards that complete grasp of form which is the final aim of all artists haunted by the ideal of perfection. Enamoured of harmony, he eliminated anatomic details, simplified his technique and circumscribed his figures within the limits of the oval or the sphere. He seemed thus to conform to the principles which govern modern sculpture in France, and cultivated with rare skill those artisan virtues which have sufficed to place among the masters a large number of second rate artists. But as soon as he foresaw the danger to his art from the breaking up of the plastic equilibrium, Jacques Lipchitz attempted a rehabilitation. To the spherical form, which was the essential basis of his work, he added the cubic formula. Light, hitherto distributed gradually over the volumes, modulated like painted surfaces, now exaggerates the differentiation of the planes in space. In elimi-

nating from his works the spherical forms which might lessen the specifically spatial character of his sculpture, Lipchitz expresses depth, not by movement but by contrast of direction. His art is objective and self-sufficient. It excludes all sentimental relation between the statue and the spectator. It is characterized by the preponderance of the cubic element. The hermetic character of Lipchitz has been much discussed. Are the statues dehumanized *a priori* and stripped of all emotional content? We do not think so. But the artist, having decided to construct architectural unities, found it necessary to convert into uniform plastic elements the constituent part of the heterogenous bodies which he represented. Thus the hair, the flesh, and the draperies of a stone woman, instead of being differentiated realistically, form an homogenous organism, determined by the laws of the medium out of which they are created. Each fragment of such a work though incorporated in the whole, has assigned to it a special rôle independent of its representative value. On the other hand, its principle of economy imposes on the artist certain constructive processes such as the interpenetration of adjoining planes, whose object is to reduce to the minimum repetitions in the body. In binding contiguous masses Jacques Lipchitz achieves organic unity. The need for full expression has always been one of his gravest preoccupations.

"Lipchitz' statues mean nothing but themselves. They are accessible only to those who show themselves capable of disassociating the plastic from the representative element, those who appreciate a work of art exclusively for artistic reasons."

6 Marion Lorillard's impression of the studio at Boulogne-sur-Seine, in *Paris-Comet*, February 1929.

"We would pass through the little garden adorned by Lipchitz' statues which, like all 'stones,' love the green of moss and ivy and are loved by them.

"If we were lucky enough to find her at home Berthe Lipchitz, who looks like a bright Russian doll, would give us coffee in a small ship-shape room filled with ship models and with prints and paintings of frigates in full sail.

"And then we would surprise Jacques working in one

or another of his big studios with his big dog Maraud, who looks like an Early Christian lion, curled up somewhere near him.

"... We would take our leave of Jacques and Berthe, who would press us hospitably to come again to lunch next time, when they would make us Russian dishes and show us Jacques' fine collection of Russian stones and African sculptures and old French iron work."

7 Jacques Baron, in *Documents*, 1930.

"And Lipchitz works on his own, though not without noticing what is happening in this world swarming with phantoms. He is aware instinctively, sees the reefs and avoids them. But I have only just realized that he has not only great gifts but also great patience. All that is the fruit of profound and intense effort, of wide knowledge and an austere craft. No, these are no monsters, these statues proudly erected in honor of nature, they are the work of a man who observes the gestures of life with fine, calm eyes; the work of a man with muscles of steel, a sound heart, clear understanding, such as is needed by the future."

8 Bernard Colrat, on an exhibition at the Galerie de la Renaissance, in *La Renaissance*, June 1930.

"Lipchitz says, 'Even if I wished to do otherwise, I could not. At the moment I am only able to make monsters.' And before making 'monsters' he was only able to make these simple architectural masses to which he gives neither name nor subject, or these ornamental reliefs in the manner of Braque (if one may separate the idea 'Braque' from the idea 'painting')."

9 E. M. Benson, in the *American Magazine of Art*, August 1935.

"Cubism for him was not a formula, a passkey to every door, but a point of view and he never worked it to death. Each new piece of sculpture represented new problems which he solved, without equivocation, freshly and ingeniously.

"... Lipchitz found that from the point of view of sculptural organics, the geometry of man and bird was indistinguishable (Brancusi made this discovery about the same time); that the physical laws which determined human anatomy also controlled plant and animal morphology and that it was the sculptor's job to translate these universal laws into organic, sculptural terms rather than their naturalistic equivalents. His mother and child stone carving which he finished in 1930 heralded this new direction. When he showed this sculpture to me he said: 'I should like to see this standing before a maternity hospital.' This is clearly not the wish of a studio sculptor. He was beginning to think in terms of the great masses of humanity outside the four walls of his workshop.

"...As Lipchitz explained it [his *David and Goliath*] to a reporter for a Paris daily, 'My Jewish skin has tingled for my scattered and persecuted blood-brothers. But the monster whom we are killing is not merely anti-Semitism, it is as well everything which hinders man from moving forward.'"

10 Juan Larrea, in the *College Art Journal*, Summer 1954.

"...As a consequence, plastic art, which had become a morphology receptive to any sort of request, begins in your hands to constitute a language or system for the transmission of signs....

"Apropos of the above aims, it does not strike me as an insignificant coincidence, *first*, that your revolutionary work is marked by your having begun by sculpturing a *Head* in 1915, an extremely novel head—comparable perhaps to the cubing 'noosphere'—that upper part of the body lacking in Rodin's precursory *Walking Man*; *second*, that Maurice Raynal should have written the following words about that head which, relating them to certain of my foregoing affirmations, I wish to recall to you. 'It is a stone head dated 1915 that marks the starting point of the sculptural renaissance initiated by Lipchitz. The poet that he is before becoming the bearer of great messages that he will be, invokes light and space as divinities whose benefits are desired, but divinities created by man, as it should be and as should never be forgotten. The work then will be a new personage living by its own life. To accomplish this kind of miracle, it was only necessary to canalize the two

formidable motions of space and light within those impassable limits whose placing remains the secret of the Masters.'"

11 Robert Goldwater, in *Lipchitz*. New York, 1959 (written 1954).

"Lipchitz has remarked that he has never been subject to the romanticism of the fragment, so essential for Rodin. Neither has he employed the romanticism of the pantheistically evolving natural material from which the figure is seen emerging. In Lipchitz' work these are conveyed by the open intricacy of the formal relations, and by the multiple reference of many of the symbols....

"The transparencies of the twenties thus continue to have their effect upon two decades of Lipchitz' sculpture. Besides, both in form and technique they have had an important influence upon a whole school of younger European and American artists, who in the last few years have been exploring the possibilities of fluid open metal construction."

12 Albert Elsen, in the *College Art Journal*, Spring 1958.

"To supplement the inheritance of twentieth century art, as well as the legacy of Rodin, Lipchitz has drawn heavily upon his Jewish background. Whereas Rodin's religious art or spiritual themes derive from the Western European Catholic tradition and ancient Hellenism, Lipchitz' art is strongly rooted in the Old Testament and Jewish traditions, along with his interest with the occult and in religious customs of early societies. Rodin's views inclined more towards the Greek anthropomorphic tradition. Some of Lipchitz' imagery is closer to the spirit of primitive idols with their crude power and mystical, awesome presence. Such sculptures as *Prayer* and *Sacrifice* are formed of values that are supramundane and correspond to the apprehension of the physical world found in primitive societies. His *Virgin of Assy* is not a goddess of the Renaissance, but belongs rather to some early medieval cult."

Biographical data

1891 On 22nd August birth of the first child, Chaim Jacob, to Rachel Leah Krinsky and her husband Abraham Lipchitz at Druskieniki (Lithuania) situated in a wooded region on the Nemen river. His father is a building contractor and comes from a rich banking family.

1902–9 Begins very early to draw and to model in clay and bread. Attends commercial school in Bialystok until 1906, when his parents send him to high school in Vilna as a safety measure after a pogrom against the Jews. After Lipchitz takes final examination, his father wants him to be trained as an engineer. Supported by the advice of a sculptor, Professor Ginzberg, the assistant of the Russian sculptor, Antokolsky, Lipchitz' mother decides to send him to Paris, illegally and without his father's knowledge. He arrives in Paris October 1909.

1909–10 Becomes a "free pupil" at the École des Beaux-Arts under Jean Antoine Ingalbert, lives at the Hôtel des Mines, Boulevard St. Michel. His father gives up his opposition. Lipchitz enters a small class and learns to carve directly in stone. Attends the sculpture classes of Raoul Verlet at the Académie Julian, wins a first prize and a medal; also attends an evening class in drawing and a general course at the Académie Collarossi and for two years studies anatomy under Dr. Richet at the École des Beaux-Arts. Sees much art in museums and collections, studies art history, with a preference for Archaic Greek, Egyptian, and Gothic art. Begins collecting passionately.

1911 The allowance from home stops due to a decline in the family business. A fellow pupil, Bernard Szeps, aids him even when he develops tuberculosis; recuperates in Belgium. On his return lives with Césare Sofianopulo at 51, Rue de Montparnasse. This is the first studio of his own.

1912–13 Is recalled to Russia for military service but, discharged on medical grounds, returns to Paris in the autumn, now to a studio at 54, Rue de Montparnasse, next door to Brancusi. He begins exhibiting in small galleries, at the Salon d'Automne with *Woman and Gazelles*, and at the Salon National des Beaux-Arts. Contacts with the Cubist painters are encouraged by his friend Diego Rivera. He becomes friends with Max Jacob, Modigliani, Soutine, and especially Picasso, which results in many exchanges of ideas and a long friendship.

1914 Majorca with Rivera and Marie Blanchard, then Madrid where he exhibits *Woman with Pigtails* and works in a gallery. At the Prado Museum he discovers the great painters, especially El Greco, Hieronymous Bosch, Tintoretto, and Goya. Returns to Paris in December.

1915 Meets, and later marries, the Bessarabian poetess, Berthe Kitrosser. A full acceptance of Cubist possibilities takes place, and he is on the way toward powerful abstraction. Makes detachable constructions.

1916 Becomes close friend of Juan Gris. Work attracts general attention. Léonce Rosenberg signs a contract with him and he can now take assistants. At Gris's house he sees much of Gertrude Stein, Reverdy, and the Chilean poet, Huidobro. Creates a sensation by cutting a hole through a figure.

1918 At Gris's insistence, Lipchitz, Gris, Metzinger, and Marie Blanchard, leave Paris, which is threatened by bombardment, for Beaulieu-près-Loches. He cannot do much sculpting but draws more than usual and makes reliefs. They return in the Autumn. The very young writer Radiguet and Jean Cocteau, of whom he was to make portraits, join the circle of his friends.

1920 The fruit of ten years in Paris are exhibited at Léonce Rosenberg's. However, he buys back his sculpture and makes himself entirely free of his contract. Maurice Raynal publishes a monograph about him. Waldemar George and other art critics begin to follow his work.

1922 The purchase of sculpture by the well-known Dr. Albert C. Barnes and his commissioning of bas-reliefs for the Barnes Foundation at Merion near Philadelphia are important for him.

1924–25 Lipchitz becomes a French citizen, marries Berthe Kitrosser, and asks Le Corbusier to build him a house and studio in the then still rural Boulogne-sur-Seine. A new period begins with the first of the "transparents" in which he makes ingenious use of the cire-perdue process.

1926 17-year-old brother, Rubin, comes to Paris for further education, at first lives with Jacques, later studies at Strasbourg. It is he, especially after 1945, who looks after Jacques's interests after he settles in America.

1927 Freed from too rigorous a Cubism by the transparents, he begins to create more fluid, rounded forms, as in the *Joie de Vivre*, commissioned by the Vicomte Charles de Noailles for his garden at Hyères. Juan Gris dies.

1928 His father dies, then his beloved sister, Genia. Death makes a deep impression on him and influences his creative activity. Commissions continue: firedogs for Jacques Doucet at Auteuil and a garden figure for Madame de Mandrot at Le Pradet.

1930 A hundred works are exhibited in the Galerie de la Renaissance (Jeanne Bucher). The large human motifs of the Return of the Prodigal Son and the Mother and Child develop. World events begin to have their effect on him.

1931 The *Song of the Vowels* for Madame de Mandrot at Le Pradet is begun and is completed in 1932 (now in the Kunsthaus, Zurich). Another issue is in the Musée d'Art Moderne, Paris, and a third is in a private collection, New York.

1934 His mother dies.

1935 First large exhibition of his work in America at the Brummer Gallery, New York. Introduction to the catalogue by Elie Faure.

1936–38 A large Prometheus sculpture for the World's Fair in Paris and motifs of struggle with monsters (*Rape of Europa, Bull and Condor*) give his work a menacing and troubled character under the pressure of current events. The *Prometheus* is designed for one of the entrances to the Palais de la Découverte et des Inventions, housed in the Grand Palais. The Petit Palais devotes a whole room to his work in the exhibition *Les maîtres de l'art indépendant*.

1939–41 The German advances compel him in 1940 to leave Paris and go to Toulouse. He has felt himself restricted for some years but he continues to do much drawing and makes portraits until, under pressure from American friends, he decides to come to America, and makes the journey with Berthe by boat via Portugal. Has lost his collection and most of his own work (except a portfolio of drawings and a few other things). Settles at 42 Washington Square South, New York.

1942 Curt Valentin manages to set him on his feet again and an exhibition follows in Valentin's Buchholz Gallery, 57th Street. Lipchitz finds a studio at 2 East 23rd Street near Madison Square. (After Curt Valentin's death in 1954, Fine Arts Associates New York, become his agents.)

1943–44 Works on a commission, *Prometheus Strangling the Vulture*, from the Ministry of Health and Education, Rio de Janeiro. (Due to misunderstanding, the sculpture is cast to the size of the model instead of being enlarged to three times the size, according to Lipchitz' plan.)

1946–47 Returns to Paris with Berthe. Large exhibition at Galerie Maeght. Important commission from Father Couturier for a baptismal font for the church at Assy, Haute-Savoie, *(Notre Dame de Liesse)*. Berthe remains in Paris. He returns to New York and establishes himself at Hastings-on-Hudson, surrounded by magnificent natural scenery not too far from New York City. He is made a Chevalier de la Légion d'Honneur.

1948 Marries Yulla Halberstadt. Birth of a daughter, Lolya Rachel. His sculptures reveal in their motifs signs of the tensions to which his life is subject. He now begins the series of the studies for the *Notre Dame de Liesse*.

1950–51 The Birth of the Muses is the theme for a large bas-relief, preceded by many studies, for Mrs. John D. Rockefeller, III. The studies for *Notre Dame de Liesse* at Assy lead in 1951 to the execution of a large model. Receives important commission for Fairmount Park, Philadelphia.

1952 On January 5th studio in 23rd Street burns down, which involves the loss of the large model for Assy, the study for Philadelphia, and much of what he had produced in America. American museums launch an aid committee which enables him to start again and to build a studio at Hastings-on-Hudson designed by Philip L. Goodwin and Martin Lowenfish. Temporarily uses a studio at Modern Art Foundry in Long Island City.

1953 Moves into the new studio at Hastings-on-Hudson and resumes work on the great projects for Assy and the *Spirit of Enterprise* for Philadelphia.

1955–56 Much important work produced, including the semi-automatics, portraits, and themes partly saved from the fire, such as *Mother and Child* and *Hagar in the Desert*.

1958 Awarded an honorary doctorate by Brandeis University, Waltham, Massachusetts.

1959 A serious illness interrupts work for several months. Makes a series of fantastic bronzes from small objects (e.g., wood, flowers, wire, rope, etc.) which push the cire-perdue technique to its limits. Series exhibited at the Fine Arts Associates, New York, under the title *A la limite du possible*.

Bibliography

The excellent bibliography published in Henry R. Hope, *The Sculpture of Jacques Lipchitz*, New York, The Museum of Modern Art, 1954, has served as the basis for this bibliography, with grateful acknowledgment of the author.

Statements and writings by Lipchitz

1 *Valori Plastici* (Rome) v. 1, nos. 2–3, Feb.-Mar. 1919, p. 3. (Brief quotation in letter from Léonce Rosenberg to the editor of *Valori Plastici* explaining Cubism)
2 "Questionnaire," *The Little Review* (New York) v. 12, May 1929, p. 47–48, port.
3 *Omaggio a Modigliani*. Milan, 1930.
4 "Réponse à une enquête sur l'art d'aujourd'hui," *Cahiers d'Art* (Paris) v. 10, 1935, p. 68, illus.
5 "The Story of My *Prometheus*," *Art in Australia* (Sydney) ser. 4, no. 6, June–Aug. 1942, p. 29–35, illus., port.
6 *Bronzes by Degas, Matisse, Renoir*. New York, Buchholz Gallery, Curt Valentin, 1943. (Foreword to exhibition catalogue)
7 *Juan Gris*. New York, Buchholz Gallery, Curt Valentin, 1944. (Exhibition catalogue)
8 *Symposium on "Guernica" ... November 25, 1947*, New York. The Museum of Modern Art, 1947. (Typescript in the Library of the Museum of Modern Art, New York)
9 "I Remember Modigliani," *Art News* (New York) v. 49, Feb. 1951, p. 26–29, 64–65, illus. (As told to Dorothy Seckler)
10 *Fourteen Eyes in a Museum Storeroom*. Philadelphia, University Museum Bulletin, University of Pennsylvania, Feb. 1952. (Lipchitz selects anthropological objects from the Museum storeroom)
11 *Amedeo Modigliani* (Library of Great Painters, Portfolio Edition). New York, Harry N. Abrams, 1952, 22 pp., illus.
12 "What in the World? Identification of Archaeological Objects: A Television Broadcast," *Archaeology* (Cambridge, Mass.) v. 6, Mar. 1953, p. 18–23, port.
—See also 42, 58, 64, 66, 67, 69, 76.

Books and articles about Lipchitz

13 Bissière. "Lipchitz," *Action* (Paris) no. 4, 1920, p. 39–42, illus.
14 Raynal, Maurice. *Lipchitz* (Art d'Aujourd'hui). *Action*, (Paris) 1920, 15 pp., 21 plates
15 Salmon, André. "Des Indépendants au Louvre," *Europe Nouvelle* (Paris) v. 3, Feb. 14, 1920, p. 281.
16 Dermée, Paul. "Lipchitz," *Esprit Nouveau* (Paris) no. 2, Nov. 1920, p. 169–182, illus., port.
17 George, Waldemar. "Jacques Lipchitz," *Amour de l'Art* (Paris) v. 2, 1921, p. 255–258, illus.
18 George, Waldemar. "La sculpture de Jacques Lipchitz," *Vie des Lettres* (Paris) v. 4, Apr. 1921, p. 490–491, illus.
19 George, Waldemar. Sculpteurs d'aujourd'hui: "Jacques Lipchitz," *Sélection* (Brussels) v. 2, Nov. 1921, p. 16–21, illus.
20 "The Sculpture of Jacques Lipchitz," *Vanity Fair*, Dec. 1922, p. 51, illus., port.
21 Cocteau, Jean. "Jacques Lipchitz and My Portrait Bust," *Broom* (Rome) v. 2, 1922, p. 207–209, illus.
22 "The Technique of Jacques Lipchitz," *Broom* (Rome) v. 2, 1922, p. 216–219, illus.
23 George, Waldemar. "Jacques Lipchitz," *Das Kunstblatt* (Berlin) v. 6, 1922, p. 58–64, illus.
24 Kuhn, Alfred. *Die neuere Plastik*. Munich, Delphin-Verlag, 1922, p. 126–127, illus.
25 George, Waldemar. "Jacques Lipchitz," *Feuilles Libres* (Paris) v. 4, Dec. 1922-Jan. 1923, p. 429–430.
26 George, Waldemar. "Jacques Lipchitz," *Gazette des Arts*, Sept. 1923, p. 10, illus.
27 George, Waldemar. "La Fondation Barnes," *Amour de l'Art* (Paris) v. 4, 1923, p. 601–604, illus.
28 Levinson, A. "Sculpteurs de ce temps," *Amour de l'Art* (Paris) v. 5, 1924, p. 390–391, illus.
29 Hildebrandt, Hans. *Die Kunst des 19. und 20. Jahrhunderts*. Waldpark-Potsdam, Athenaion, 1924, p. 443, illus.
30 Parkes, Kineton. "The Constructional Sculpture of Jacques Lipchitz," *The Architect* (London) v. 114, Sept. 18, 1925, p. 202–204, illus.
31 George, Waldemar. "Bronzes de Jacques Lipchitz," *Amour de l'Art* (Paris) v. 7, 1926, p. 299–302, illus.

32 Salmon, André. "Jacques Lipchitz," *Art d'Aujourd'hui*, (Paris) v. 3, no. 10, 1926, p. 21–23, illus.

33 Salmon, André. "La sculpture vivante," *L'Art Vivant* (Paris) May, 1926, p. 335.

34 Einstein, Carl. *Die Kunst des 20. Jahrhunderts*. Berlin, Propyläen-Verlag, 1926, p. 173, 547–549, 570, illus.

35 Stein, Gertrude. "Lipchitz," *Ray* (London) no. 2, 1927, p. 1.

36 George, Waldemar. *Jacques Lipchitz*. Paris, Le Triangle [1928?] 17 pp., 18 plates. (Text in Yiddish)

37 Huidobro, Vicente. "Jacques Lipchitz," *Cahiers d'Art* (Paris) v. 3, 1928, p. 153–158, illus.

38 Ozenfant, Amédée. *Foundations of Modern Art*, New York, Dover, 1952, p. 104–108, illus. (First published in French, 1928.)

39 Brielle, Roger. "Jacques Lipchitz," *Sud Magazine* (Marseilles) Sept. 1929, p. 9–11, illus.

40 Lozowick, Louis. "Jacques Lipchitz," *Menorah Journal* (New York) v. 16, 1929, p. 46–48, illus.

41 Zervos, Christian. "Notes sur la sculpture contemporaine," *Cahiers d'Art* (Paris) v. 4, 1929, p. 465–473, illus.

42 Vitrac, Roger. *Jacques Lipchitz* (Les sculpteurs français nouveaux, 7). Paris, Librairie Gallimard, 1929, 63 pp., illus. (Includes statements by Lipchitz)

43 Lorillard, Marion. "Jacques Lipchitz: There Is Something in Modern Art After All," *Paris-Comet*, Feb. 1929, p. 47–49, illus.

44 Colrat, Bernard. "Jacques Lipchitz," *La Renaissance* (Paris) v. 13, June, 1930, p. 149–154, illus.

45 Baron, Jacques. "Jacques Lipchitz'" *Documents* (Paris) v. 2, no. 1, 1930, p. 17–26, illus.

46 Tériade, E. "A propos de la récente exposition de Jacques Lipchitz," *Cahiers d'Art* (Paris) v. 5, 1930, p. 259–265, illus.

47 Huidobro, Vicente. "Lipchitz," in Edouard-Joseph, R. (ed.). *Dictionnaire biographique des artistes contemporains, 1910–1930*. Paris, Art & Edition, 1931, v., 2, p. 398–399, illus.

48 Vitrac, Roger. "Jacques Lipchitz, Sculptor," *The Bulletin* (American Women's Club of Paris, Inc.) Jan. 1931, p. 275, illus.

49 Guéguen, Paul. "Jacques Lipchitz; ou, L'histoire naturelle magique," *Cahiers d'Art* (Paris) v. 7, 1932, p. 252–258, illus.

50 Fierens, Paul. *Sculpteurs d'aujourd'hui*. Paris, Editions des Chroniques du Jour, 1933, p. 14–15, illus.

51 Benson, E. M. "Seven Sculptors," *The American Magazine of Art* (Washington, D.C.) v. 28, Aug. 1935, p. 454–481, illus.

52 Craig, Martin. "Jacques Lipchitz," *Art Front* (New York) v. 2, Jan. 1936, p. 10–11, illus. (Review of the exhibition at the Brummer Gallery).

53 Torres García, J. "El escultor Jacques Lipchitz," *Tribuna Cultural* (Montevideo) May, 1936, p. 24–30, illus.

54 Giedion-Welcker, Carola. *Contemporary Sculpture*. New York, Wittenborn, 1955, p. 50–57, illus. (A revised and enlarged edition of *Modern Plastic Art*, 1937)

55 Zervos, Christian. *Histoire de l'art contemporaine*. Paris, Editions "Cahiers d'Art," 1938, p. 297, 305–306, 308, illus.

56 *12 dessins pour Prométhée, 1940*. Paris, Jeanne Bucher [1941?] 12 colorplates in portfolio.

57 Schwartzberg, Miriam B. *The Sculpture of Jacques Lipchitz*. New York, New York University, 1941, 136 pp. 29 plates. (Typescript of thesis in the Library of the Museum of Modern Art, New York)

58 Georges-Michel, Michel. *Peintres et sculpteurs que j'ai connus, 1900–1942*. New York, Brentano's, 1942, p. 282–283. (Report of a conversation with Lipchitz)

59 Hartley, Marsden. "Letter to Jacques Lipchitz," in his *The Spangle of Existence* [1942] p. 194–197. (Typescript in the Library of the Museum of Modern Art, New York)

60 Gómez de la Serna, Ramón. "Lipchitzmo," in his *Ismos*. Buenos Aires, Editorial Poseidon, 1943, p. 231–236, illus.

61 *Twelve Bronzes by Jacques Lipchitz*, New York, Buchholz Gallery, Curt Valentin, 1943, 2 pp., 16 plates. (Exhibition catalogue)

62 Rewald, John. "Jacques Lipchitz's Struggle," *The Museum of Modern Art Bulletin* (New York) v. 12, Nov. 1944, p. 7–9, illus.

63 *The Drawings of Jacques Lipchitz*. New York, Buchholz Gallery, Curt Valentin, 1944, 3 pp., 20 plates.

64 Sweeney, James Johnson. "An Interview with Jacques Lipchitz," *Partisan Review* (New York) v. 12, Winter 1945, p. 83–89.

65 Jacques Lipchitz: Sculptures exécutés aux Etats-Unis," *Cahiers d'Art* (Paris) v. 20–21, 1945–1946, p. 394–404. (Illustrations only)

66 Sweeney, James Johnson. "Eleven Europeans in America," *The Museum of Modern Art Bulletin*, v. 13, Sept. 1946, p. 24–27, 38, illus.

67 Warnod, André. "Jacques Lipchitz," *Arts* (Paris) no. 95, Nov. 29, 1946, p. 5. (An interview)

68 Rewald, John. "Lipchitz retourne en France," *Arts* (Paris) no. 73, June 21, 1946, p. 4.

69 "A Little Song," *Time* (New York) v. 47, Feb. 18, 1946, p. 63, illus. (Includes statement by Lipchitz on his *Benediction*)

70 Raynal, Maurice. "La sculpture de Jacques Lipchitz," *Arts de France* (Paris) no. 6, 1946, p. 43–50, illus.

71 Guéguen, Pierre. "Retour d'un sculpteur," *Architecture d'Aujourd'hui* (Paris) v. 16, May–June, 1946, p. 92–93, illus.

72 Pach, Walter. "Lipchitz and the Modern Movement," *Magazine of Art* (Washington, D.C.) v. 39, Dec. 1946, p. 354–359, illus.

73 Cassou, Jean. "Lipchitz," *Horizon* (London) v. 14, Dec. 1946, p. 377–380, illus.

74 Raynal, Maurice. *Jacques Lipchitz*. Paris, Editions Jeanne Bucher, 1947, 17 pp., 72 plates, port. (Reproductions cover the period 1911 to 1945)

75 "Lipchitz," in *Current Biography*, 1948, v. 9, New York, H. W. Wilson, 1949, p. 378–380, port.

76 Sweeney, James Johnson. "Two Sculptors: Lipchitz and Arp," *Theatre Arts* (New York) v. 33, Apr. 1949, p. 52–56, illus. (An interview)

77 Dorival, Bernard. "Un An d'activité au Musée d'Art Moderne," *Musées de France* (Paris) no. 1, Jan.–Feb. p. 18–19, illus.

78 Frost, Rosamund J. "Lipchitz Makes a Sculpture," *Art News* (New York) v. 42, Apr. 1950, p. 36–39, 63–64.

79 Weller, Paul. "Jacques Lipchitz: A Portfolio of Photographs," *Interiors* (New York) v. 109, May 1950, p. 88–95, illus.

80 Slusser, Jean Paul. "Sculptures by Arp and Lipchitz," *Bulletin* (University of Michigan Museum of Art, Ann Arbor) v. 1, no. 1, May, 1950, p. 9–12, illus. (Discussion of Lipchitz' *Happiness*)

81 Coutrier, M. A. "Assy," *Art Sacré* (Paris) no. 1–2, Sept.–Oct. 1950, p. 1–20, illus.

82 Faure, Elie. "Jacques Lipchitz et le cubisme," *Arts Plastiques* (Brussels) no. 2, 1950, p. 117–122, illus. (Article written 1932–33)

83 George, Waldemar. "Jacques Lipchitz, père légitime des transparents," *Art et Industrie* (Paris) v. 27, no. 24, 1952, p. 28–29, illus.

84 "Fire," *Art Digest* (New York) v. 26, Feb. 1, 1952, p. 14. (On the destruction of Lipchitz' studio, Jan. 2)

85 Bouret, Jean. "Lipchitz, le constructeur," *Arts* (Paris) no. 345, Feb. 8, 1952, p. 4.

86 "Another Phoenix," *Art Digest* (New York) v. 26, Feb. 15, 1952, p. 13, illus. (Lipchitz' *Sacrifice* acquired by the Albright Art Gallery)

87 Kelleher, Patrick J. "Additions to the Permanent Collection: *Sacrifice* by Jacques Lipchitz," *Gallery Notes* (The Buffalo Fine Arts Academy, Albright Art Gallery) v. 16, May–October, 1952, p. 2–3.

88 Hope, Henry R. "La scultura di Jacques Lipchitz," *Biennale* (Venice) no. 10, Sept. 1952, p. 8–11, illus.

89 Veronese, Giulia. "Jacques Lipchitz," *Emporium* (Bergamo) v. 116, nos. 691–692, July–Aug. 1952, p. 53–56, illus.

90 Auerbach, Arnold. *Sculpture: A History in Brief*. London Elek, 1952, p. 85–87, 101, illus.

91 Ritchie, Andrew Carnduff. *Sculpture of the Twentieth Century*. New York, The Museum of Modern Art, 1953, p. 32, 42–43, 178–181, illus.

92 Goldwater, Robert. *Jacques Lipchitz*. New York, Universe Books, 1959, 18 pp., 33 plates. (First issued in Dutch, 1954)

93 Couzijn, W. "In de Werkplaats van Lipchitz," *Kroniek van Kunst en Kultuur* (Amsterdam) v. 14, Jan. 1954, p. 1–2, illus., port.

94 Braat, L. P. J. "Lipchitz; het Wezen van zijn Werk," *Kroniek van Kunst en Kultuur* (Amsterdam) v. 14, Jan. 1954, p. 2–3, illus.

95 Larrea, Juan. "An Open Letter to Jacques Lipchitz," *College Art Journal* (New York) v. 13, no. 4, Summer 1954, p. 251–288, illus.

96 Hope, Henry, R. *The Sculpture of Jacques Lipchitz*. New York, The Museum of Modern Art, 1954. 95 pp., illus.
(Catalogue of the exhibition)

97 Elsen, Albert. "The Humanism of Rodin and Lipchitz," *College Art Journal* (New York)
v. 17, no. 3, Spring 1958, p. 247–265, illus.

98 Nelson, James (ed.). *Wisdom: Conversations with the Elder Wise Men of Our Day*. New York, W.W. Norton & Company, 1958, p. 263–273, illus. (Transcript of a television conversation)

Exhibitions

1911 Paris. First exhibition, in a gallery probably called Gil Blas on the Boulevard Malesherbes near the Place St. Augustin.

1912 Paris. Takes part in the Salon d'Automne and the Salon National des Beaux-Arts.

1914 Madrid. An exhibition with Diego Rivera and Marie Blanchard.

1920 Paris. First large one-man exhibition, organized by Léonce Rosenberg.

1930 Paris. Retrospective exhibition of 100 sculptures at the Galerie de la Renaissance, organized by Jeanne Bucher. Catalog.

1935 New York. Brummer Gallery. Catalog with text by Elie Faure.

1937 Paris. Petit Palais. Catalog (*Les Maîtres de l'Art Indépendant*) includes 36 works by Lipchitz.

1942 New York. Buchholz Gallery, Curt Valentin. Catalog.

1943 New York. Buchholz Gallery, Curt Valentin. Catalog

1946 New York. Buchholz Gallery, Curt Valentin. Catalog.
Paris. Galerie Maeght. Catalog with text by Jean Cassou, Camille Soula, Jacques Kober.

1948 New York. Buchholz Gallery, Curt Valentin. Catalog.

1950 Portland. Oregon Art Museum. Catalog with text by Andrew C. Ritchie. (Also shown at San Francisco Art Museum and Cincinnati Art Museum in 1951). Brussels. Petite Galerie du Séminaire. Drawings.

1951 New York. Buchholz Gallery, Curt Valentin. Catalog includes list of sculptures by Lipchitz owned by American museums.
New York. Exhibition circulated by Museum of Modern Art: *Birth of the Muses*.

1952 Venice. 26th Biennale. Catalog includes 22 works by Lipchitz.
Beverly Hills, California. Frank Perls Gallery. Catalog. (Also shown at Santa Barbara Museum.)

1954 New York. Museum of Modern Art. Illustrated catalog with introduction by Henry R. Hope. (Also shown at the Walker Art Center, Minneapolis and the Cleveland Museum of Art.)

1957 Exhibitions at Cincinnati; Fine Arts Associates, New York, and Frank Perls Gallery, Beverly Hills, California.

1958–59 Amsterdam. Stedelijk Museum. An exhibition of 116 works (1911–1957) selected by the sculptor himself. Illustrated catalog. Subsequently shown at Otterlo (Rijksmuseum Kröller-Müller), Basel, Dortmund, Paris, Brussels, and London.
New York. Fine Art Associates. Entitled *A la limite du possible*. Catalog with illustrations and the artist's introduction to new works.

Drawings and sculptures

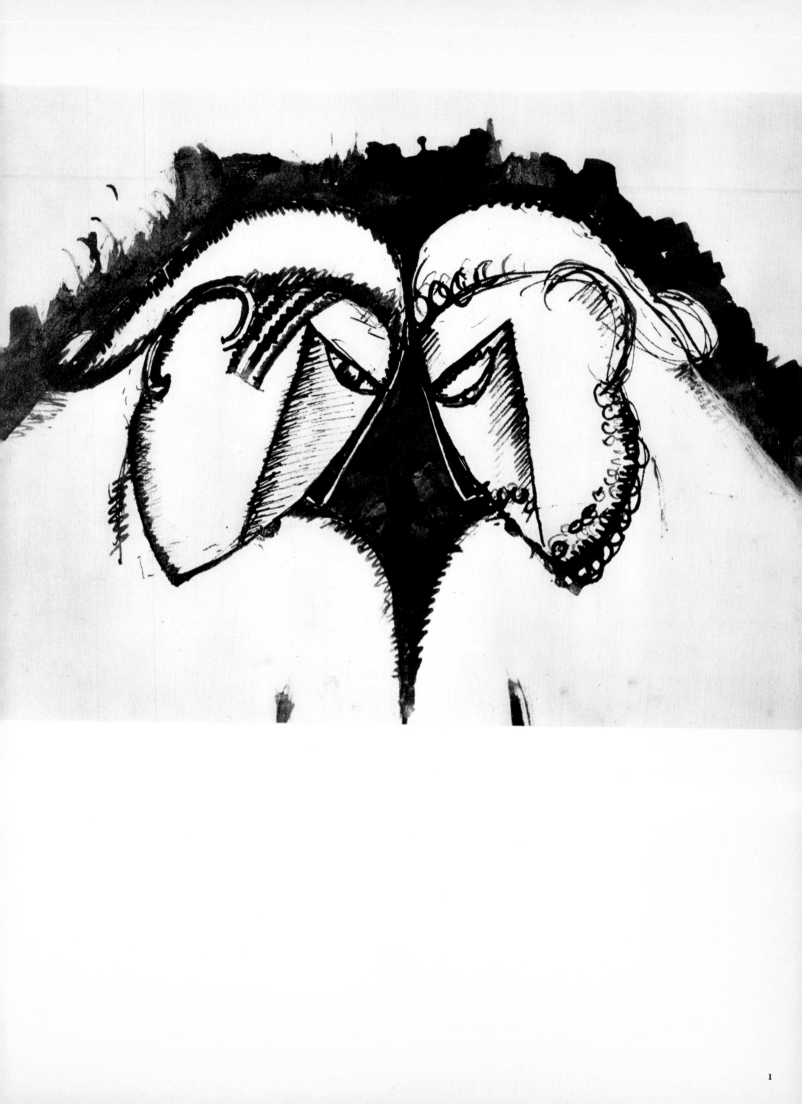

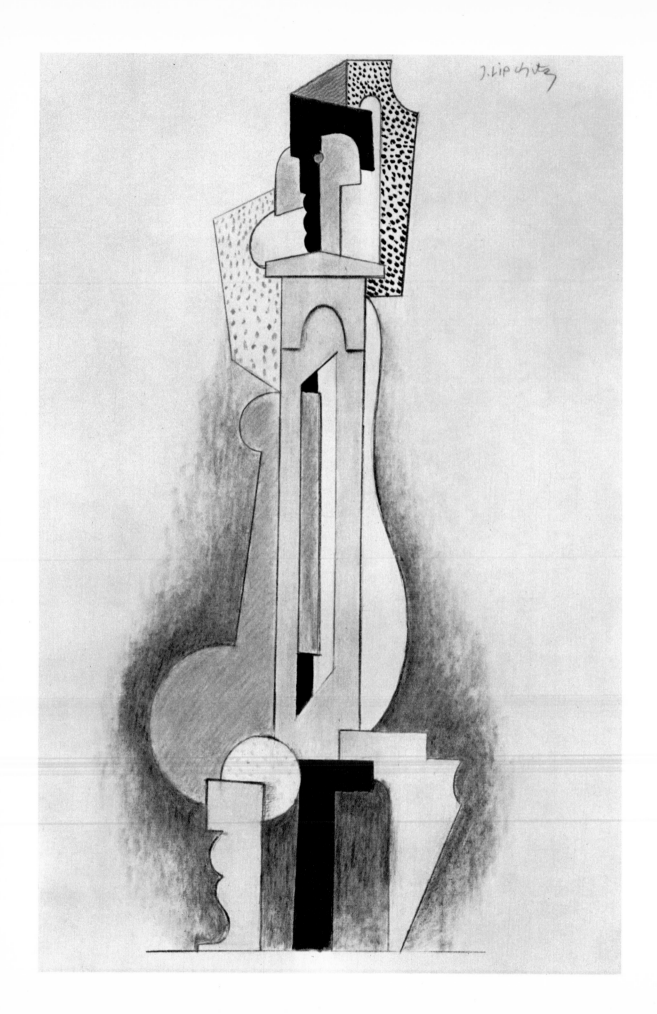

4

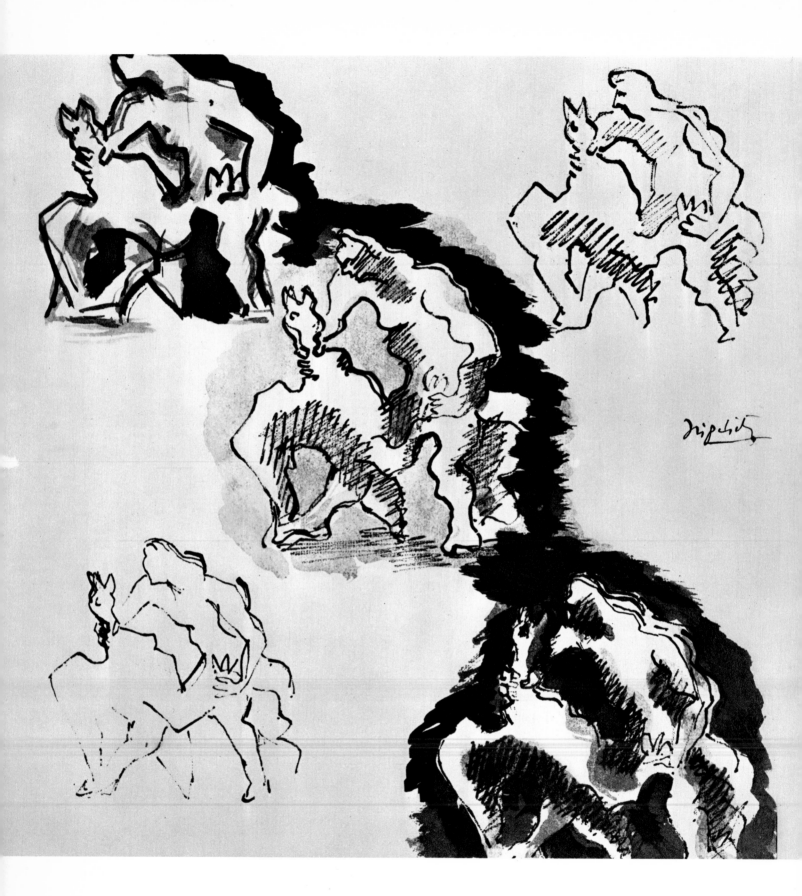

8

13   14

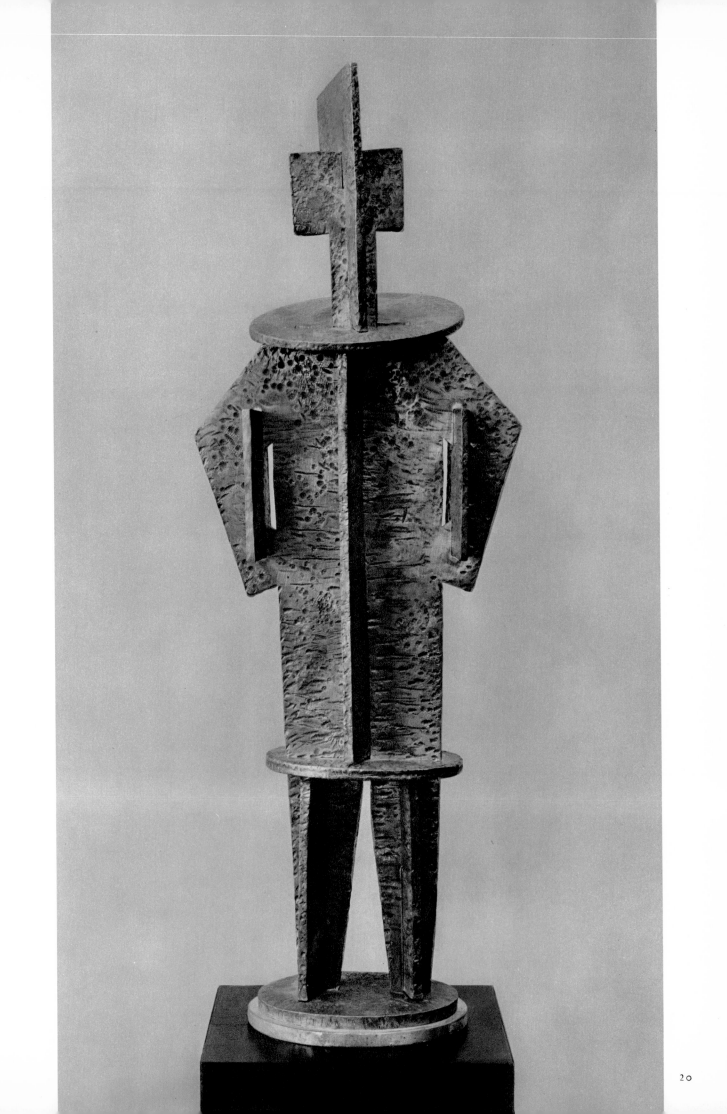

20

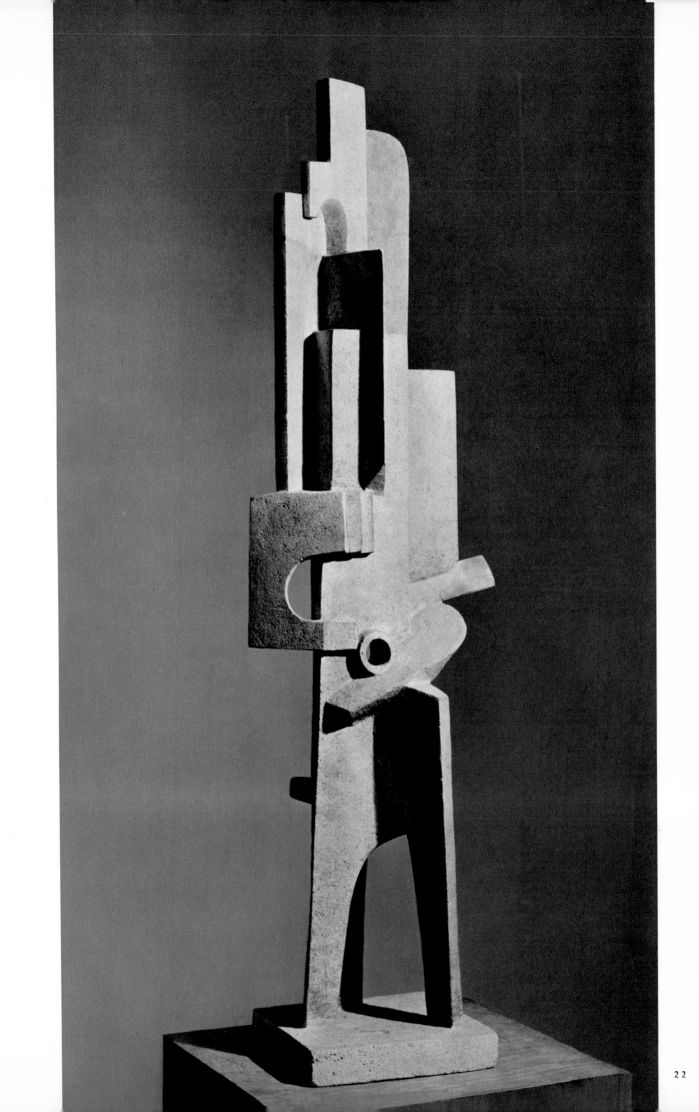

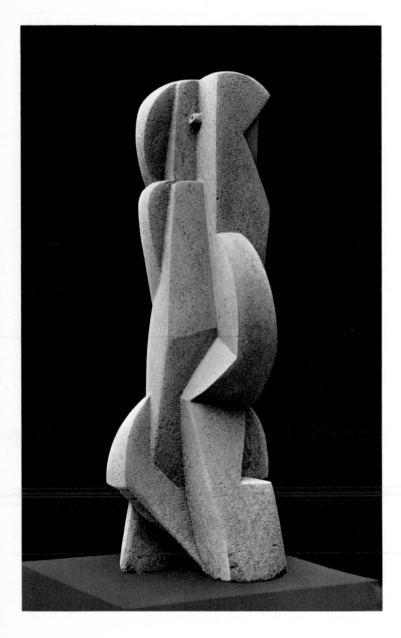 

28   29   30

35

36

42

47

48

52　　　　　　　　53

62

63

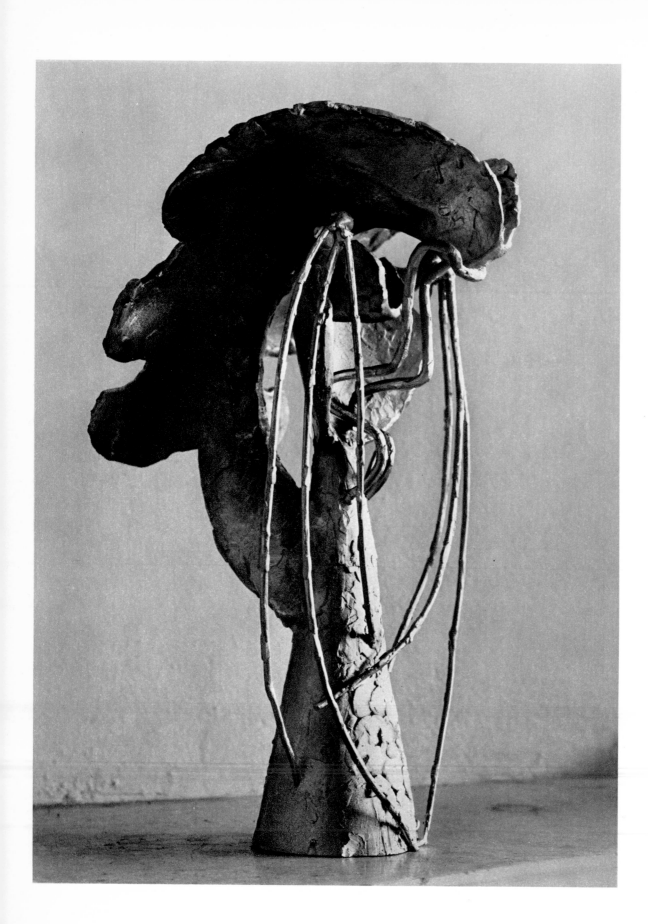

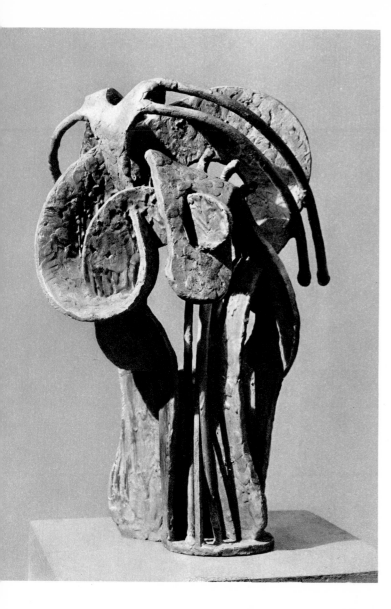

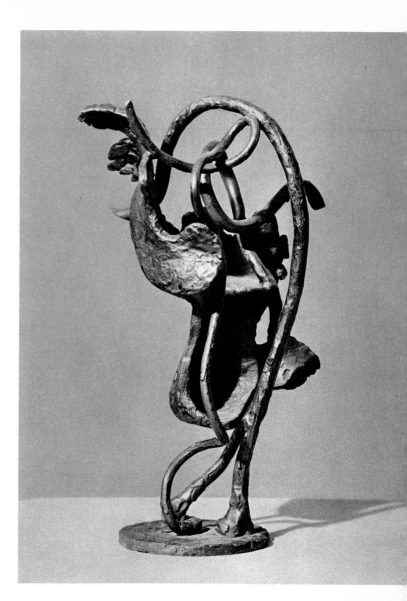

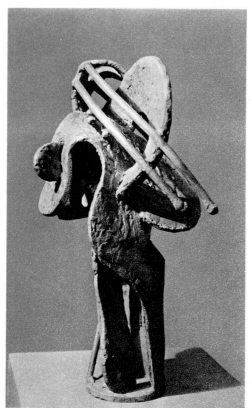

70

71

72

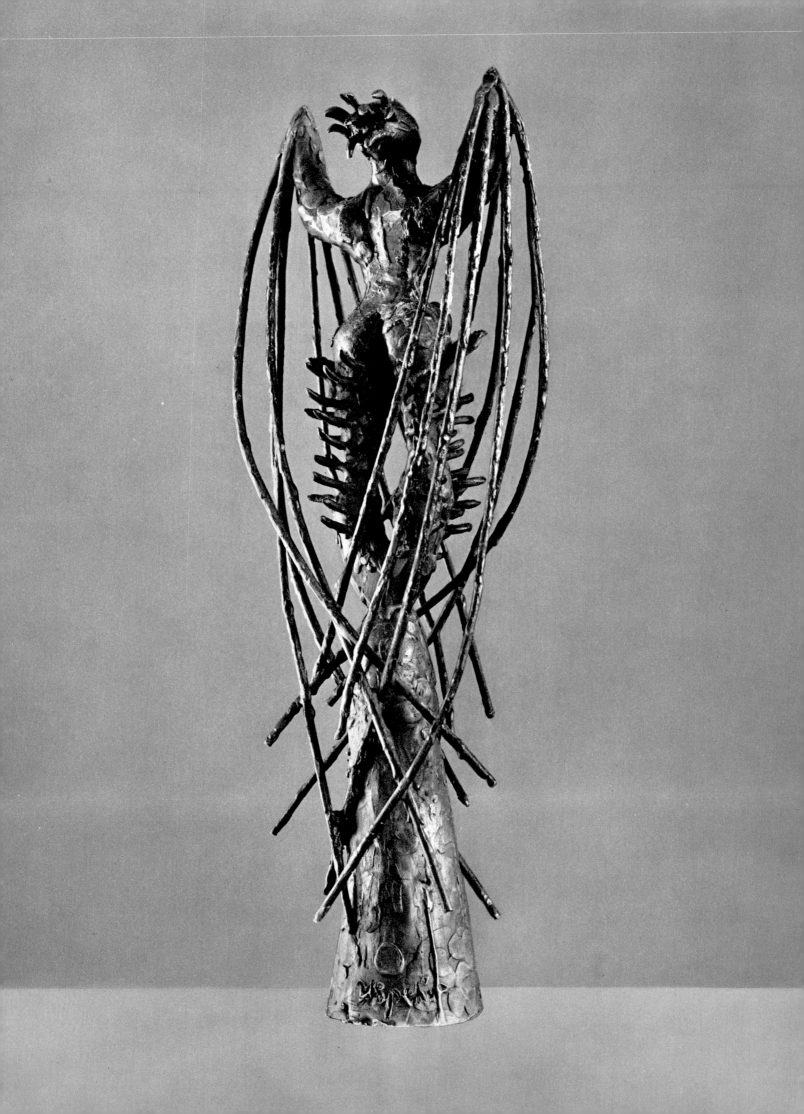

79

80

91/92 93/94

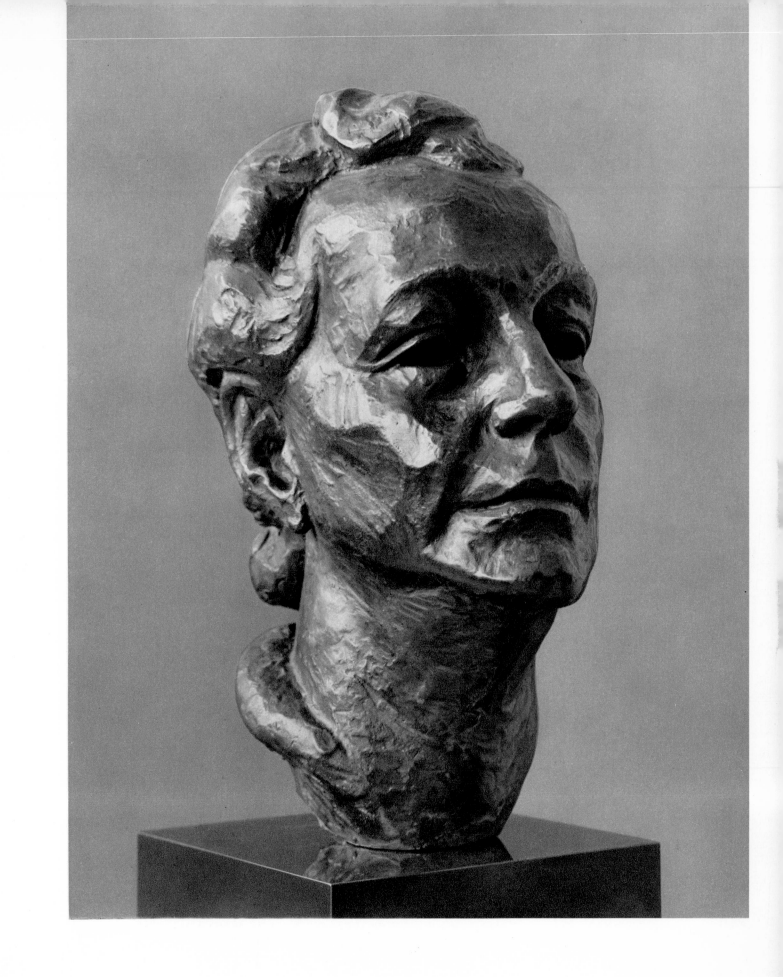

List of reproductions

Documentation, stylistic development, subject matter

Data are given in as detailed a form as possible though in some cases particular facts were not available. Unless otherwise stated, the measurements refer to the height.

I Lipchitz as a child

II Lipchitz' mother, age 32

III Lipchitz' father

IV Lipchitz, age 21

V Lipchitz, age 21

VI Seated Nude, *1910. First Prize and medal of the Académie Julian, Paris*

VII The Poet and Painter Cesare Sofianopulo, *1911. Bronze, life-size. Collection Cesare Sofianopulo, Trieste*

VIII Lipchitz in 1922

IX Lipchitz in 1926, in the garden of his house, built by Le Corbusier, Boulogne-sur-Seine

X Studio of the house at Boulogne-sur-Seine

XI Lipchitz *(drawing by Modigliani)*, *1916. 12½ × 9″. Collection Jacques Lipchitz*

XII Lipchitz *(drawing by Modigliani)*, *1916. 12½ × 9″. Collection Jacques Lipchitz*

XIII Lipchitz *(drawing by Modigliani)*, *1916. 12½ × 9″. Collection Jacques Lipchitz*

XIV *Front of a postcard from Lipchitz to Giovanni Scheiwiller, 1921*

XV *Back of postcard from Lipchitz to Giovanni Scheiwiller, 1921*

XVI *Lipchitz in Paris in 1937, with the clay model of his* Prometheus Strangling the Vulture, *commissioned for the Paris World's Fair*

XVII *Studio at 2 East 23rd Street, New York, 1944*

XVIII *Lipchitz at Hastings-on-Hudson working on the bronze statue of* Notre Dame de Liesse

XIX *The new studio, built on a cliff above the river at Hastings-on-Hudson, into which Lipchitz moved in 1953*

XX *Studio at Hastings-on-Hudson, January 1959*

XXI *Lipchitz, January 1959*

XXII *The plaster model for* La Joie de Vivre *(1927), in the studio at Hastings-on-Hudson*

XXIII Woman with Serpent, *1913. Bronze, 25″. Philadelphia Museum of Art*

XXIV Dancer, *1913. Bronze, 24″. Collection Mr. and Mrs. Bernard J. Reis, New York*

XXV Acrobat on Horseback, *1914. Bronze, 21¾″. Otto Gerson Gallery, New York*

XXVI Head, *1915. Bronze, 24½″. Collection Joseph Hirshhorn, New York*

XXVII Bather III, *1917. Stone, 28½″. Barnes Foundation, Merion, Pennsylvania*

XXVIII Standing Figure, *1916. Stone, 49¾″. Owned by the artist*

XXIX Man with a Guitar, *1916. Stone, 38¼″. The Museum of Modern Art, New York (Mrs. Simon Guggenheim Fund)*

XXX Bather, *1915. Bronze, 38½″. Mrs. John D. Rockefeller III, New York*

XXXI Harlequin with Accordion, *1918, Stone, 30"*. *Present owner unknown*
XXXII Seated Bather, *1919. Stone, 28½"*. *Barnes Foundation, Merion, Pennsylvania*
XXXIII Recumbent Woman *(model for a firedog)*, *1922. Bronze, 14"*. *Collection Mlle. Gabrielle Chanel, Paris*
XXXIV Seated Man, *1922. Granite, 20"*. *Virginia Museum of Fine Arts, Richmond*
XXXV Seated Bather, *1924. Clay, 15½"*. *Collection Mrs. Dolly Chareau*
XXXVI Seated Man, *1925. Onyx, 14½"*. *Collection Mr. and Mrs. William Mazer, New York*
XXXVII Harlequin with Banjo, *1926. Bronze. Present owner unknown*
XXXVIII The Harpists, *1930. Bronze, 18"*. *Collection Mr. and Mrs. Bernard J. Reis, New York*
XXXIX The Harp Player, *1928. Bronze, 10½"*. *Collection Mrs. T. Catesby Jones, New York*
XL Reclining Nude with Guitar, *1928. Black stone, 26⁷⁄₈" long. Collection Mrs. John D. Rockefeller III, New York*
XLI Return of the Prodigal Son, *1931. Bronze, 44"*. *Owned by the artist*
XLII Prometheus Strangling the Vulture, *1943–44. Plaster, 100"*. *Owned by the artist*
XLIII Spring, *1942. Bronze, 14"*. *Collection Mr. & Mrs. Bernard J. Reis, New York*
XLIV The Joy of Orpheus, *1945. Bronze, 20½." Owned by the artist*
XLV Sacrifice III, *1949–57. Bronze, 49¼"*. *Collection Mr. and Mrs. Ted Weiner, Fort Worth, Texas*
XLVI Femme Fleur, *1956. Bronze, 11¼"*. *Otto Gerson Gallery, New York*
XLVII The Meeting, *1913. Plaster, 31½"*. *Owned by the artist*
XLVIII The Couple, *1929. Plaster, 37½"*. *Rijksmuseum Kröller-Müller, Otterlo, The Netherlands*
IL The Embrace, *1934. Bronze, 19½"*. *Owned by the artist*
L Song of Songs, *1946. Bronze, 24"*. *Collection Mrs. Henry R. Hope, Bloomington, Indiana*
LI Mother and Children, *1914–15. Bronze, 28¾"*. *Owned by the artist*
LII Mother and Child, *1929–30. Plaster, 56"*. *Owned by the artist*
LIII *Study for* "Mother and Child," *1931. Terra cotta, 4½"*. *Owned by the artist*
LIV Mother and Child II, *1941–45. Bronze, 50"*. *The Museum of Modern Art, New York (Mrs. Simon Guggenheim Fund)*
LV Mother and Child, *1948. Bronze, 15½"*. *Owned by the artist*
LVI Hagar II, *1949, Bronze, 13¼"*. *Owned by the artist*
LVII Hagar in the Desert, *1957. Bronze, 35"*. *Collection Mr. and Mrs. Ted Weiner, Fort Worth, Texas*
LVIII *Study for* "David and Goliath," *1930. Terra cotta, 30¾"*. *Owned by the artist*
LIX Prometheus and the Vulture, *1936. Bronze, 18"*. *Collection Mr. & Mrs. Sam Jaffe, Beverly Hills, California*
LX Rape of Europa, *1938. Bronze, 23⅛" long. Collection Mr. Michael Zagajski, New York*
LXI Theseus, *1942. Bronze, 25¼"*. *Owned by the artist*

Drawings and sculptures

1 The Meeting, *1912. Drawing in India ink. Collection Miss Helen M. Harding, New York*

2 Study for a Sculpture, *1915. Drawing in pencil, crayon, and India ink. Collection J. Tucker, St. Louis*

3 Study for a Sculpture, *1916. Conté, Collection Joseph Hayden, New York*

4 Study for a Polychrome Bas-Relief, *1918. Tempera on panel. Present owner unknown*

5 Study for a Polychrome Bas-Relief, *1918. Tempera on panel. Present owner unknown*

6 Benediction *(study), 1943. Distemper on panel, $27\frac{3}{4} \times 21\frac{1}{4}"$. Owned by the artist*

7 A Couple *(study), 1944. Distemper on panel, $17\frac{3}{4} \times 21\frac{1}{4}"$. Collection Mr. & Mrs. Richard S. Davis, Wayzata, Minnesota*

8 Prometheus *(study), 1936–37. Drawing in India ink, $13\frac{1}{4} \times 12\frac{1}{4}"$. Owned by the artist*

9 Gazelle, *1911. Bronze, 18". Collection Madame Le Mée, Paris*

10 Woman with Serpent *(front view), 1913. Bronze, 25". Philadelphia Museum of Art*

11 Woman with Serpent *(front view)*

12 The Meeting, *1913. Lead, $31\frac{1}{2}"$. Owned by the artist*

13 Dancer, *1913. Bronze, 24". Collection Mr. and Mrs. Bernard J. Reis, New York*

14 Horseman with Fan, *1913. Bronze, $27\frac{1}{2}"$. Owned by the artist*

15 Sailor with Guitar, *1914. Bronze, 32". Musée d'Art Moderne, Paris*

16 Bather III *(side view), 1917. Stone, $28\frac{1}{2}"$. Barnes Foundation, Merion, Pennsylvania*

17 Bather III *(back view)*

18 Bather III *(front view)*

19 Mother and Children, *1914–15. Bronze, $28\frac{3}{4}"$. Owned by the artist*

20 Detachable Figure, *1915. Bronze, $27\frac{1}{4}"$. Collection Robert Bollt, New York*

21 Head, *1915. Bronze, $24\frac{1}{2}"$. Collection Joseph Hirshhorn, New York*

22 Man with a Guitar, *1916. Stone, $38\frac{1}{4}"$. The Museum of Modern Art, New York (Mrs. Simon Guggenheim Fund)*

23 Bather, *1915. Bronze, $38\frac{1}{2}"$. Collection Mrs. John D. Rockefeller III, New York*

24 Dancer, *1915. Ebony and oak, $39\frac{1}{4}"$. Owned by the artist*

25 Bather, *1919. Bronze, 28". Collection Miss Jane Wade, New York*

26 Sailor with Guitar, *1917–18. Bronze, 36". Owned by the artist*

27 Draped Woman, *1919. Bronze, $37\frac{1}{2}"$. Collection Mr. and Mrs. Ted Weiner, Fort Worth, Texas*

28 Bather, *1916. Stone, 30". Present owner unknown*

29 Seated Bather, *1917. Stone, 30". Collection Mr. and Mrs. Ralph F. Colin, New York*

30 Bather, *1923–25. Bronze, 80". Otto Gerson Gallery, New York*

31 Portrait of Gertrude Stein, *1920. Bronze, $13\frac{1}{2}"$. The Detroit Institute of Arts*

32 Portrait of Raymond Radiguet, *1920. Bronze, 12". Owned by the artist*

33 Seated Man, *1925. Onyx, 14½". Collection Mr. and Mrs. William Mazer, New York*

34 Seated Man with Guitar, *1922. Granite, 15⅞". Collection Nelson A. Rockefeller, New York*

35 Still Life *(relief), 1918. Bronze, 20½ × 28½". Collection Mr. and Mrs. Andrew Gagar, Litchfield, Connecticut*

36 Musical Instruments *(relief), 1924. Bronze, 19¼". Collection Mrs. Dolly Chareau, New York*

37 Harlequin with Mandolin *(relief), 1924–25. Bronze, 50". Owned by the artist*

38 Pierrot Escapes, *1926, Bronze, 18¼". Kunsthaus, Zurich*

39 Harlequin with Guitar, *1926. Bronze, 13¼". Formerly collection Jeanne Bucher, Paris*

40 The Harp Player, *1928. Bronze, 10½". Collection Mrs. T. Catesby Jones, New York*

41 Elle, *1931. Bronze, ca. 10¼". Private collection, United States*

42 Chimène, *1930. Bronze, 18". Owned by the artist*

43 Ploumanach, *1926. Bronze, 30¾". Collection Mrs. Werner Baer, Zurich*

44 Reclining Nude with Guitar, *1928. Black stone, 26⅞" long. Collection Mrs. John D. Rockefeller III, New York*

45 Figure *(side view), 1926–30. Bronze, 85¼". The Museum of Modern Art, New York (Van Gogh Purchase Fund) (Photo taken in park of Rijksmuseum Kröller-Müller, Otterlo, The Netherlands)*

46 Figure *(front view)*

47 La Joie de Vivre, *1927. Plaster, 88". Owned by the artist*

48 La Joie de Vivre, *1927. Bronze 89¼". Collection the Vicomte Charles de Noailles, Hyères, France*

49 The Couple, *1929. Bronze, 28". Rijksmuseum Kröller-Müller, Otterlo, The Netherlands*

50 Return of the Prodigal Son, *1931. Bronze, 44". Owned by the artist*

51 Mother and Child, *1930. Bronze, 56". The Cleveland Museum of Art (Stone Memorial Fund and Bernard J. Reis)*

52 Hands, *1933. Bronze, 21¼". Owned by the artist*

53 The Harpists, *1930. Bronze, 20⅞". Collection Mrs. T. Catesby Jones, New York*

54 Song of the Vowels, *1931–32, Bronze, 80". Collection Nelson A. Rockefeller, New York*

55 Woman Leaning on Elbows, *1933. Bronze, 27½". Owned by the artist*

56 Head, *1932. Bronze, 9". Stedelijk Museum, Amsterdam*

57 Monument (Toward a New World), *1939. Bronze, 46". Collection Messrs. Sikkens, Leiden*

58 Portrait of Géricault *(after his death mask), 1933. Bronze, 24". Musée des Beaux-Arts, Rouen, France*

59 Rape of Europa, *1941. Bronze, 34". Collection R. Sturgis Ingersoll, Penllyn, Pennsylvania*

60 Rape of Europa, *1938. Bronze, 23⅛" long. Collection Mr. Michael Zagajski, New York*

61 Prometheus Strangling the Vulture, *1943–44. Plaster, 100". Owned by the artist*

62 Prometheus and the Vulture, *1936. Bronze, 18". Collection Mr. and Mrs. Sam Jaffe, Beverly Hills, California*

63 Prometheus Strangling the Vulture II, *1944–53. Bronze, 100". Philadelphia Museum of Art*

64 Mother and Child *(back view). First casting. Collection Edgar J. Kaufmann, photographed at Falling Water (architect: Frank Lloyd Wright), Bear Run, Pennsylvania*

65 Mother and Child *(side view)*

66 Mother and Child II *(front view), 1941–45. Bronze, 50". The Museum of Modern Art, New York (Mrs. Simon Guggenheim Fund)*

67 Spring, *1942. Bronze, 14". Collection Mr. and Mrs. Bernard J. Reis, New York*

68 Blossoming, *1941–42. Bronze, 21½". The Museum of Modern Art, New York (Given anonymously)*

69 Barbara, *1942. Bronze, 15⅝". Smith College Museum of Art, Northampton, Massachusetts*

70 Trentina, *1946. Bronze, 20". Collection Mrs. Lois Orswell, Pomfret Center, Connecticut*

71 Trentina *(side view)*

72 Variation, *1942. Bronze, 16". Owned by the artist*

73 Myrah, *1942. Bronze, 23¼". Owned by the artist*

74 The Promise, *1942. Bronze, 18". Collection Dr. H. Kayden, New York*

75 The Pilgrim, *1942. Bronze, 29¾". Owned by the artist*

76 Prayer, *1943. Bronze, 42½". Collection R. Sturgis Ingersoll, Penllyn, Pennsylvania*

77 Benediction I, *1942. Bronze, 42". Collection Mr. and Mrs. Bernard J. Reis, New York*

78 Benediction I, *(side view)*

79 The Rescue, *1945. Bronze, 16". Collection Dr. J. van der Wal, Amsterdam*

80 Song of Songs, *1946. Bronze, 24". Collection Mrs. Henry R. Hope, Bloomington, Indiana*

81 Dancer with Braids, *1947. Bronze, 14¼". Owned by the artist*

82 Dancer with Hood *(side view), 1947. Bronze, 16¼". Owned by the artist*

83 Dancer with Hood *(side view)*

84 Mother and Child, *1948. Bronze, 15½". Owned by the artist*

85 Pastorale, *1947. Bronze, 22". Owned by the artist*

86 Hagar *(study), 1948. Cast stone, 10½". Collection Miss Jane Wade, New York*

87 Hagar, *1948. Bronze, 32¾". Art Gallery of Toronto, Canada*

88 Mother and Child, *1949. Bronze, 52". Otto Gerson Gallery, New York*

89 *Study for* "Notre Dame de Liesse," *1950. Bronze, 33". Owned by the artist*

90 Miracle II, *1947. Bronze, 30¾". Jewish Museum, New York*

91 Centaur *(variation on a chisel), 1952. Gilded bronze, 7½". Collection Mr. G. David Thompson, Pittsburgh*

92 Woman with a Bird *(variation on a chisel)*, *1952. Bronze, 10". Collection Mr. Saul Rosen, Paterson, New Jersey*

93 The Poet *(variation on a chisel)*, *1952. Bronze, 9". Owned by the artist*

94 Combat *(variation on a chisel)*, *1952. Bronze, 10". Owned by the artist*

95 Hebrew Objects *(variations on a chisel)*, *1951. Bronze, ca. 8¾". Collection S. Schocken, Scarsdale, New York*

96 Portrait of Leib Jaffe, *1944. Bronze, 15¼". Museum, Tel Aviv*

97 Portrait of Mrs. John Cowles, *1956. Bronze, 16". Collection Mr. and Mrs. John Cowles, Minneapolis*

98 Sacrifice III, *1949–57. Bronze, 49¼". Collection Mr. and Mrs. Ted Weiner, Fort Worth, Texas*

99 Souvenir de Loie Fuller, *1955–56. Bronze, 10". Owned by the artist*

100 Sketch for "Enterprise," *1953. Bronze, 31¼". Tate Gallery, London*

Photographic sources

Colten Photos, New York: 96
Gemeente Musea van Amsterdam: LXI
George Moffet (Lensgroup), New York: XVIII
Philadelphia Museum of Art: XLII, 63
Hans Sibbelee: XLI, LI, LIV, LVII, LIX, LX, 9, 12, 19, 26, 30, 32, 45, 46, 49, 50, 51, 52, 54, 55, 56, 57, 58, 60, 62, 66, 73, 75, 80, 87, 88, 100,
Star Press of New York: 20
Adolph Studly, New York: XXIX, XXX, XLIII, XLIV, XLV, XLVI, L, LVI, 1, 2, 3, 4, 5, 6, 7, 8, 21, 22, 23, 24, 25, 27, 28, 29, 31, 33, 34, 40, 41, 42, 43, 44, 53, 59, 61, 64, 65, 67, 68, 69, 70, 72, 74, 77, 78, 79, 81, 82, 83, 84, 85, 86, 90, 91, 92, 93, 94, 95, 97, 98, 99
Marc Vaux Paris: X, XI, XII, XIII, XVI, XXIII, XXIV, XXV, XXVI, XXVII, XXXIV, XXXV, XXXVI, XXXVIII, XXXIX, XL, XLVII, XLVIII, IL, LII, LVIII, 10, 11, 13, 14, 15, 16, 17, 18, 35, 36, 37, 38, 39, 47, 48

Acknowledgments

The first essential in order to produce this book, which was started in 1957, was the full approval and co-operation of Jacques Lipchitz. As far as the earlier work is concerned, his extensive *œuvre* was still in the studio at Boulogne-sur-Seine. The later work is in the studio at Hastings-on-Hudson. Rubin Lipchitz in Paris was always ready with help and the answers to countless questions. In America Jacques Lipchitz, on the various occasions I had the privilege of talking with him, supplied in his own typically warm and generous manner all those details that are indispensable to a writer if his work is to reflect something of the man and his *œuvre*. Numerous letters in that characteristically expressive handwriting later carried on the discussion. Miss Jane Wade and Dr. Otto M. Gerson of the Fine Arts Associates placed at my disposal all their records, including those of the former Curt Valentin Gallery in New York, for the documentation of the works. Some details could not be traced. The foundations laid by Henry R. Hope in his catalogue *The Sculpture of Jacques Lipchitz*, published by the Museum of Modern Art, New York (April, 1954), proved of great value. Mr. G. P. de Neve, Director of the Contact publishing house, and Mrs. K. Vranken were responsible for the supervision of the whole, while the typographer, Otto Treumann, took great pains with the graphic design. At the conclusion of this work I should like to express my deep gratitude to all of them for their help.

A. M. HAMMACHER